Abu Dhabi
Top 10

100+ of Abu Dhabi's very best must-sees and must-dos

there's more to life...
ask**explorer**.com

Abu Dhabi Top 10
1st Edition 2013
2nd Edition 2015

Published by Explorer Publishing & Distribution
PO Box 34275
Dubai UAE
+971 (4) 340 8805
retail@ask**explorer**.com
explorerpublishing.com

Front cover photograph
Al Meena Dhows – Hardy Mendrofa

To buy additional copies of this or any other of Explorer's award-winning titles visit
explorerpublishing.com/shop. Special discounts are available for quantity purchases.

ISBN 978-1-78596-000-0 – Al Meena Dhows

National Media Council Approval No. #134

Printed and bound in Dubai by Emirates Printing Press

Welcome...

...to **Abu Dhabi Top 10**, your step-by-step guide to the UAE's capital. Abu Dhabi is both the UAE's biggest emirate and its capital city – making it a must-see destination for anyone living in or visiting the region.

Whether you're looking for city attractions or outdoor adventures, fine dining or the best beaches, this book is your handy guide to the emirate's essential experiences. In total, we've listed 100 of Abu Dhabi's very best, divided into 10 categories that range from supreme showstopper restaurants to essential family days out, from cracking cultural attractions to the best bars in the city – and plenty more in between. From number one to number 10, they're in no particular order, so make sure you try to get around as many as possible.

And, as we always like to give our readers that little bit extra, you'll also find the top 10 places to visit outside of Abu Dhabi as well as lists of the top 10 malls, 10 not-to-miss golf courses and 10 child-friendly restaurants and cafes that the whole family will love.

So, whether you're visiting Abu Dhabi for a day, a week, a month, or maybe even longer, there's no excuse for not seeing the very best that the city, and the United Arab Emirates, has to offer.

For even more inspiration, **askexplorer.com** is jam-packed with tips for the latest happenings and openings in the UAE and beyond.

Happy exploring,

The Explorer Team

We'd love to hear from you, whether you make a great insider discovery or want to share your views about this or any of our products. Get in touch with us at askexplorer.com or through any of our social media channels.

YAS ISLAND YOUR TICKET TO A WORLD OF MAGIC

only few things age better with time...

GMP

www.graymackenzie.com

Contents

ask**explorer**.com

Since 1996, **explorer** has been the UAE's number one source on living life to the fullest under the Gulf sun.

With some 150 much-loved products in our portfolio, we cover every aspect of life in the Middle East: from off-road adventures to career advice, there's a guide to match all interests – get yours today at **askexplorer.com/shop**.

And for even more insider tips and inspiration, including details of the latest happenings in Abu Dhabi, Dubai and beyond, **askexplorer.com** has all the answers.

Sheikh Zayed Grand Mosque

Welcome To
Abu Dhabi

The thriving cosmopolitan capital in the heart of the Middle East offers architectural splendour, opulent luxury, high-octane thrills and a fascinating heritage.

The island city of Abu Dhabi is a lush, modern metropolis that has a lot to offer visitors with its tree-lined streets, futuristic skyscrapers, huge shopping malls and international luxury hotels. The city is surrounded by the sparkling azure waters of the Arabian Gulf, a striking contrast to the large parks and green boulevards across the urban island. And, as you'd expect from a truly international destination, there is a wide scope of activities, cuisines and adventures to be found.

Culture & Heritage

Culture

Abu Dhabi is a melting pot of many nationalities and cultures and the city's effort to become modern and cosmopolitan is proof of an open-minded and liberal outlook. There's a healthy balance between western influences and eastern traditions here and the emirate is still very rooted in its heritage.

Modern Abu Dhabi

People & Economy

The UAE population has grown rapidly in recent years as expat arrivals, robust economic expansion and high birth rates push up the number. According to The World Factbook, the UAE's population stood at around 9.2 million in 2014, with the capital's population estimated at 2.3 million. The UAE Statistics Bureau has, in the past, calculated that the country's population has shot up by as much as 65% over the past five years to reach its latest figure and topping nine million.

The UAE is one of the world's richest countries thanks to its oil wealth and diversification strategy. In 2014, Abu Dhabi was seeing year-on-year growth in non-oil sectors, 15% growth in airport traffic, and an increase in the production capacity of hydrocarbons, and is on target for its Abu Dhabi Economic Vision 2030 (abudhabi.ae).

Investment & Free Trade Zones

Abu Dhabi is one of the top investment-attracting countries in the world. The free trade zones in the capital are a major attractor, and the first financial free zone, the Abu Dhabi Global Market Square on Al Maryah Island opened in early 2015. Benefits to businesses in free zones include 100% foreign ownership, which negates the usual need for local partner sponsorship where a UAE national or entity owns at least 51%. They also get tax exemptions and 100% repatriation of revenue and profits.

Tourism

With the capital's increase in hotels, sporting events and new attractions, the emirate has become a major tourist destination in its own right.

New Developments

Billions of dirhams are being invested to transform the city into the cultural capital of the Arab world and many key projects focus on art, design and architecture. Yas Island is home to Yas Marina Circuit (home to the Formula 1 Grand Prix), Ferrari World, Yas Waterworld, and the new Yas Mall. The Louvre Abu Dhabi and the Guggenheim Abu Dhabi will open in the next few years on Saadiyat Island.

Visiting Abu Dhabi

Getting There
Abu Dhabi International Airport is undergoing a major expansion and redevelopment programme. Terminal 3, exclusively for Etihad flights, opened in 2009 and more additions are on the way.

Airport Transfers
If you book your break through a hotel or travel agency, it's likely that pick-up from the airport will be included. If not, there is a regular bus service between Abu Dhabi International Airport and Abu Dhabi city centre. The fully air-conditioned, green and white bus number A1 runs every 40 minutes, 24 hours a day, from outside the arrivals halls of Terminals 1, 2 and 3. The fare is Dhs.4, however you will need to pay by cash as cards are not accepted. If you have flown into Dubai, there is also a shuttle bus that will bring you over to Abu Dhabi.

Visas & Customs
Requirements vary depending on your country of origin and it's wise to check the regulations before departure. GCC nationals (Bahrain, Kuwait, Qatar, Oman and Saudi Arabia) do not need a visa to enter Abu Dhabi. Citizens from many other countries get an automatic 30-day visa upon arrival at the airport. You can renew this for a further 30 days at a cost of Dhs.500.

Certain medications, including codeine, Temazepam and Prozac, are banned even though they are freely available in other countries

The UAE has a zero tolerance policy towards drugs. Even a miniscule quantity in your possession could result in a lengthy jail term.

Local Knowledge

Climate
Abu Dhabi has a subtropical and arid climate. Sunny blue skies and high temperatures can be expected most of the year. Rainfall is infrequent, averaging only 25 days per year, mainly in winter (December to

March). Summer temperatures can hit a soaring 48°C (118°F) and with humidity well above 60% it can make for uncomfortable conditions from June to September. The best time to visit Abu Dhabi is during winter when average temperatures range between 14°C and 30°C.

Food & Drink
Common Arabic dishes are shawarma (lamb or chicken carved from a spit and served in a pita bread with salad and tahina), falafel (mashed chickpeas and sesame seeds, rolled into balls and deep fried), hummus (a creamy dip made from chickpeas and olive oil), and tabbouleh (finely chopped parsley, mint and crushed wheat).

Among the most famed Middle Eastern delicacies are dates and coffee. Dates are one of the few crops that thrive naturally throughout the Arab world. Local coffee is mild with a taste of cardamom and saffron, and it is served black without sugar.

Time
The UAE is four hours ahead of UTC (Universal Coordinated Time – formerly known as GMT). There is no altering of clocks for daylight saving in the summer. Most offices and schools are closed during the weekend, on Fridays and Saturdays. Be aware that some shops don't open until later on Fridays.

Electricity & Water
The electricity supply is 220/240 volts and 50 cycles. Most hotel rooms and villas use the three-pin plug that is used in the UK.

Adaptors are widely available and only cost a few dirhams. Tap water is desalinated sea water and is perfectly safe to drink although most people choose mineral water because it tastes better and is cheap.

Credit Cards & Cash
Credit and debit cards are widely accepted around Abu Dhabi. Foreign currencies and travellers' cheques can be exchanged in licensed exchange offices, banks and hotels. Cash is preferred in the souks,

View From Jumeirah At Etihad Towers

markets and in smaller shops, and paying in cash will help your bargaining power. If you've hired a car, most petrol pumps will accept both cash and credit cards.

The monetary unit is the dirham (Dhs.), which is divided into 100 fils. The currency is also referred to as AED (Arab Emirate Dirham). Notes come in denominations of Dhs.5 (brown), Dhs.10 (green), Dhs.20 (light blue), Dhs.50 (purple), Dhs.100 (pink), Dhs.200 (yellowy-brown), Dhs.500 (blue) and Dhs.1,000 (browny-purple). The dirham has been pegged to the US dollar since 1980, at a mid rate of $1 to Dhs.3.6725.

Language
Arabic is the official language of the UAE, although English, Hindi, Malayalam, Urdu and Tagalog are commonly spoken. You can easily get by with English, but you're likely to receive at least a smile if you can throw in a couple of Arabic words.

Crime & Safety
Pickpocketing and crimes against tourists are a rarity in Abu Dhabi, and visitors can enjoy feeling safe and unthreatened in most places around the city. Abu Dhabi Police will advise you on a course of action in the case of a loss or theft. If you've lost something in a taxi, call the taxi company. If you lose your passport, your next stop should be your embassy or consulate. If you are crossing the road on foot, use designated pedestrian crossings (jaywalking is illegal) and, if you plan on driving, make sure you know the rules of the road. There is zero tolerance towards drink driving. Even after one drop of alcohol, you can expect a harsh penalty.

Accidents & Emergencies
If you witness an accident or need an ambulance in an emergency situation, the number to call is 999. For urgent medical care, there are several private hospitals with excellent A&E facilities. With the exception of emergency care in government hospitals, which is available for free unless you require

any follow-up treatment, you will need a health card to access government health services. For general non-emergency medical care, most hospitals have a walk-in clinic where you can simply turn up.

People With Disabilities
Abu Dhabi takes its responsibility towards visitors with special needs very seriously. Most of Abu Dhabi's five-star hotels and new buildings have wheelchair facilities and disabled parking spaces. Abu Dhabi International Airport is also well equipped for physically challenged travellers. There is a special check-in gate with direct access from the car park, as well as dedicated lifts, and a meet and assist service. Be wary though as facilities may be limited at older attractions across the capital.

Mobile & Internet
It is possible to buy SIM cards for mobile phones that work on a pay-as-you go basis from local providers, Etisalat and du. You can easily buy top-up credit for your packages from supermarkets, newsagents and petrol stations. Wi-Fi is available in many hotels and cafes around town. An Etisalat package costs Dhs.35 and is valid for 30 days. It includes 100mb of data, 25 SMS messages and 25 minutes of local and international calls. Meanwhile, du's 'Visitor Mobile Line' for Dhs.35 includes 20 SMS, 20 local and International calls and 200mb of data.

Media
Many of the major glossy magazines are available in Abu Dhabi, but if they're imported from the US or Europe, you can expect to pay at least twice the normal cover price. Most hotels have satellite or cable, broadcasting a mix of local and international channels. Catering for Abu Dhabi's multinational inhabitants, there are stations broadcasting in English, French, Hindi, Malayalam and Urdu. Most stations operate 24 hours a day and can usually be picked up with good reception throughout Abu Dhabi.

Sheikh Zayed Grand Mosque

Ferrari World

Abu Dhabi provides a fascinating mix of old and new. While the emirate is careful to preserve the traditions and culture of the past, it is also home to awe-inspiring modern architecture and record-breaking theme parks.

Abu Dhabi Golf Club

Public Holidays & Annual Events

Public Holidays

The Islamic calendar starts from the year 622AD, the year of Prophet Muhammad's migration (Hijra) from Mecca to Al Madinah. Hence, the Islamic year is called the Hijri year and dates are followed by AH (AH stands for Anno Hegirae, meaning 'after the year of the Hijra'). As some holidays are based on the sighting of the moon and do not have fixed dates on the Hijri calendar, Islamic holidays are more often than not confirmed less than 24 hours in advance.

The main Muslim festivals are Eid Al Fitr (the festival of the breaking of the fast, which marks the end of Ramadan) and Eid Al Adha (the festival of the sacrifice, which marks the end of the pilgrimage to Mecca). Mawlid Al Nabee is the holiday celebrating Prophet Muhammad's birthday, and Lailat Al Mi'raj celebrates the Prophet's ascension into heaven.

Arafat Day	24 Sept 2015 (Moon)
Eid Al Adha	25 Sept 2015 (Moon)
Islamic New Year	15 Oct 2015 (Moon)
UAE National Day	2 Dec 2015 (Fixed)
New Year	1 Jan 2016 (Fixed)
Lailat Al Mi'raj	15 May 2016 (Moon)
Eid Al Fitr	5 July 2016 (Moon)
Arafat Day	10 Sept 2016 (Moon)
Eid Al Adha	11 Sept 2016 (Moon)
Islamic New Year	1 Oct 2016 (Moon)
Mawlid Al Nabee	12 Dec 2016 (Moon)

Annual Events

Abu Dhabi hosts an impressive array of events, from Formula 1 racing and international tennis to well-respected music and film festivals. Many attract thousands of visitors, and tickets often sell out quickly.

Dhow Racing

All year round
adimsc.ae
Scheduled dhow races take place throughout the year, mostly between October and April. The event is organised by the Abu Dhabi International Marine Sports Club.

Abu Dhabi HSBC Golf Championship

January
abudhabigolfchampionship.com
There's over $2 million in prize money up for grabs, and some of the biggest names in the golfing world take part.

Abu Dhabi Festival

March-April
abudhabifestival.ae
Brings big names in classical music and fine arts every year. Brazilian musician Sérgio Mendes, conductor Riccardo Muti and violinist Anne-Sophie Mutter performed in 2015.

Abu Dhabi Desert Challenge

March-April
abudhabidesertchallenge.ae
The event attracts some of the world's top rally drivers and bike riders who compete in the car, truck and motocross categories over four days.

Al Gharbia Watersports Festival

April-May
algharbiafestivals.com
From kiteboards and surf ski kayaks among the waves to chilled-out camping and concerts, this 10-day watersports extravaganza has it all for the UAE's beach lovers. The on-shore entertainment also includes beach football and volleyball.

Powerboat Racing

October to May
adimsc.ae
Abu Dhabi International Marine Sports Club hosts races from October to May, including the final round of the season. These events include the F1 Powerboat World Championships.

Abu Dhabi Film Festival

October
abudhabifilmfestival.ae
This festival become one of the region's premier film events. Previous star-studded editions have been attended by the likes of Cate Blanchett, Uma Thurman, Clive Owen, Tilda Swinton and Richard Gere. The festival supports local and Arabic filmmakers and aims to attract more film productions to Abu Dhabi region.

Abu Dhabi Art
November
abudhabiartfair.ae
Galleries and artists from across the region and around the world converge in the airy spaces of Manarat Al Saadiyat for a full programme of installations, exhibitions, workshops and activities.

Al Ain Aerobatic Show
November-December
alainaerobaticshow.com
The five-day show features flying daredevils from all over the world displaying their incredible aerial skills with a host of aerobatic stunts.

Formula 1 Etihad Airways Abu Dhabi Grand Prix
November
yasmarinacircuit.com
As it is one of the last races of the F1 season, excitement is always guaranteed on the track, while the event also features a number of big name entertainers performing on stage at the end of each day.

Mubadala World Tennis Championship
December-January
mubadalawtc.com
After a few years of hosting the world's top male players (Federer, Nadal, Murray, Djokovic) and attracting record crowds of up to 15,000 fans, this tournament has quickly become the hottest end-of-year sporting ticket.

Getting Around

Bus
There are dozens of bus routes servicing the main residential and commercial areas of Abu Dhabi. The buses and bus shelters are air-conditioned, modern and clean, and services run more or less around the clock. Fares are inexpensive (as little as Dhs.2 for travel within the capital). The main bus station is on Hazza bin Zayed Road and there are bus stops in many of the main residential districts. 'Ojra' bus passes can be purchased at the central bus station or at any Red Crescent kiosk on the island, and an inter-urban pass costs Dhs.80 for one month of unlimited use. The front three rows of seats are reserved for women and children only. Visit ojra.ae for downloadable bus route maps.

Driving & Car Hire
Driving is on the right hand side, wearing seat belts is mandatory in the front seats, and speed limits are usually around 60 to 80kmph in town, and 100 to 120kmph on major roads. These are strictly enforced by cameras.

You will find all the major car rental companies in Abu Dhabi, plus a few local ones. It is best to shop around as rates can vary considerably.

Taxi
Taxis are reasonably priced, plentiful and the most common method of getting around. The city has a 7,000-strong taxi fleet overseen by TransAD (transad.ae). Most trips around the city shouldn't cost more than Dhs.20.

Daytime (6am-10pm) metered fares in the city start at Dhs.3.5; nighttime fares are slightly more, with the starting fare at Dhs.4 and a minimum fare of Dhs.10 after 10pm.

Walking & Cycling
Most cities in the UAE are very car-oriented and not designed to summer temperatures of more than 45°C are not conducive to a leisurely stroll. Having said that, the relative compactness of Abu Dhabi's main area makes walking and cycling a pleasant way of getting around in the cooler winter months, and an evening stroll or bike ride along the Corniche is a must. In a recent move to promote cycling, the government introduced a city bike hire scheme.

Finding Your Way Around
With new roads popping up each year, finding your way around can be made difficult. Explorer produces several of the most up-to-date city maps available, including the pocket-sized Abu Dhabi Mini Map and the handy Abu Dhabi Tourist Map; order one from askexplorer.com/shop.

Top Places To Stay

The standard of accommodation in the emirate is so high that once you've stayed in an Abu Dhabi five-star hotel, you might find luxury hotels in other parts of the world a bit disappointing. Most hotels lie on to the north of the island near the Corniche, in Al Maqtaa and on Yas Island. For a more adventurous escape, head a few hours west to the unspoilt Al Gharbia region or drive to the secluded Empty Quarter for some spectacular desert scenery.

Al Raha Beach Hotel
alrahabeach.danathotels.com
02 508 0555 **Map** p.219

Aloft Abu Dhabi
aloftabudhabi.com
02 654 5000 **Map** p.216

Courtyard By Marriott, World Trade Center
marriott.com/hotels
02 698 2222 **Map** p.213

Crowne Plaza Yas Island
ichotelsgroup.com
02 656 3000 **Map** p.222

Desert Islands Resort & Spa
desertislands.anantara.com
02 801 5400 **Map** p.210

Dusit Thani
dusit.com
02 698 8888 **Map** p.214

Eastern Mangroves Hotel & Spa By Anantara
anantara.com
02 656 1000 **Map** p.215

Emirates Palace
kempinski.com
02 690 9000 **Map** p.212

Fairmont Bab Al Bahr
fairmont.com
02 654 3333 **Map** p.217

Hilton Abu Dhabi
hilton.com
02 681 1900 **Map** p.212

Hyatt Capital Gate Abu Dhabi
hyatt.com
02 596 1234 **Map** p.216

InterContinental Abu Dhabi
intercontinental.com
02 666 6888 **Map** p.212

Jumeirah At Etihad Towers
jumeirah.com
02 811 5555 **Map** p.212

One To One Hotel The Village
onetoonehotels.com
02 495 2000 **Map** p.214

Park Hyatt Abu Dhabi Hotel & Villas
hyatt.com
02 407 1234 **Map** p.225

The Ritz-Carlton Grand Canal
ritzcarlton.com
02 818 8888 **Map** p.217

Royal Rose Hotel
royalrosehotel.com
02 672 4000 **Map** p.214

Saadiyat Beach Club
saadiyatbeachclub.ae
02 656 3500 **Map** p.227

Shangri-La Hotel, Qaryat Al Beri
shangri-la.com
02 509 8888 **Map** p.217

St Regis Saadiyat Island Resort
stregissaadiyatisland.com
02 498 8888 **Map** p.225

The Westin Abu Dhabi Golf Resort & Spa
westinabudhabigolfresort.com
02 616 9999 **Map** p.218

Tilal Liwa Hotel
danathotels.com
02 894 6111 **Map** p.210

Qasr Al Sarab Desert Resort
anantara.com
02 886 2088 **Map** p.210

Yas Viceroy Abu Dhabi
viceroyhotelsandresorts.com
02 656 0000 **Map** p.222

Saadiyat Beach Club

Despite its growing modern developments, from luxury resorts to record-breaking theme parks, Abu Dhabi has maintained strong links to its history. Within the emirate it is still possible to see reminders of centuries-old pastimes, from dhows and fortresses to traditional Islamic architecture.

Yas Viceroy

Fairmont Bab Al Bahr

معـــرض أبـوظـبي الـدولي للكتــاب
Abu Dhabi International Book Fair

ABU DHABI INTERNATIONAL BOOK FAIR

A Treasury of Knowledge at your Fingertips

ADBookFair   ADIBF

Cultural Attractions

Traditional Dhows

Cultural
Attractions
Introduction

Abu Dhabi is teeming with fascinating places to visit, many of which offer glimpses into a time when the city and emirate was nothing more than a small trading post and an endless desert.

Abu Dhabi achieves what a large number of Middle Eastern cities fail to realise: a healthy balance between western influences and eastern traditions. While the emirate is very much looking to the future, it is also very much rooted in the Islamic customs that deeply penetrate the Arabian Peninsula and beyond.

The UAE's successful effort to become modern and cosmopolitan is proof of an open-minded and liberal outlook. Consequently, the rapid economic development over the last 30 years has changed life in the emirate beyond recognition. Yet the country's rulers are committed to safeguarding their heritage and have gone to huge lengths to promote cultural and sporting events that are representative of the region's traditions. Falconry, camel racing and traditional dhow sailing are all popular, as is Arabic poetry, dancing, songs and traditional art and craftsmanship. Courtesy and hospitality are the most highly-prized virtues, and visitors are likely to experience the genuine warmth and friendliness of the Emirati people during their stay.

Abu Dhabi features many fascinating places to visit, each of which offers a glimpse into a time when the city was nothing more than a small trading port and centre for pearl diving. Many of the pre-oil heritage sites have been carefully restored, paying close attention to authentic design and using original building materials. Stroll through the Heritage Village, with its traditional-style huts and homes, and marvel at how people coped in Abu Dhabi long before air-conditioning.

The Sheikh Zayed Grand Mosque offers fascinating insights into local culture and its links to religion, while there are numerous galleries that have interesting exhibitions of art and traditional Arabic artefacts, and more are springing up all the time. Meanwhile, the Louvre Abu Dhabi, Guggenheim Abu Dhabi and Zayed National Museum will open in the next few years on Saadiyat Island.

Ramadan Timings

During the Islamic holy month of Ramadan, Muslims fast from sunrise to sunset for 30 days. The exact dates of Ramadan change every year due to the fact that Islam uses a lunar calendar (each month begins with the sighting of a new moon). As a result, Islamic holidays begin on different days with Ramadan taking place 11 days earlier each year according to the western Gregorian calendar. It is worth checking when you will be visiting Abu Dhabi, as during Ramadan, timings for many companies change significantly. Museums and heritage sites, for instance, usually open slightly later in the morning than usual, and close earlier in the afternoon.

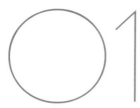

Heritage Village

Location Breakwater **Web** torath.ae
Times 9am-5pm daily, 3.30pm-9pm Fridays
Price Guide Free **Map 1** p.213

The picture postcard Heritage Village is located on the Breakwater near Marina Mall, and, facing back towards Abu Dhabi's Corniche and waterfront, the cityscape view alone is almost worth the visit. But the Heritage Village is a fascinating addition to any tourist's itinerary.

> The little spice shop is a real treat; you can buy a range of dried herbs and even handmade soap. It's also a much cheaper option for buying expensive spice saffron.

Run by the Emirates Heritage Club, it offers an interesting glimpse into the country's past. Traditional aspects of the Bedouin way of desert life, including a camp fire with coffee pots, a goats' hair tent, a well and a falaj irrigation system are displayed in the open museum. Meanwhile, there are workshops where craftsmen demonstrate traditional skills such as metalwork and pottery, while women sit weaving and spinning. The craftsmen are happy to share their skills and may occasionally give you the chance to try them out. After visiting the village, sample some Arabic cuisine at the neighbouring waterside restaurants.

Al Bateen Boatyard

Location Al Bateen, close to the InterContinental Hotel
Times Daily, except Fridays
Map 2 p.213

The Al Bateen area, on the western side of Abu Dhabi, stretches along the coast between the InterContinental hotel and Shakhbout bin Sultan St. One of the capital's most affluent areas, with plenty of green, open spaces, it has a pleasant, residential neighbourhood feel that is worlds away from the nearby city centre.

The highlight of the area is the Al Bateen Boatyard. It's here that you'll find the craftsmen who employ traditional skills to build the dhows and racing hulls that can be seen in competitions off the Corniche. The method they use has changed little over the centuries and each dhow is still a testament to the patience, technique and love of its creator. As you approach the boatyard, you'll be taken in by the evocative smells of freshly cut African and Indian teak and, if it's not too busy, the craftsmen will happily share the intricacies of their art and may even let you try your hand at dhow building. The yard is open every day except Friday and the best time to visit is around 5pm.

Be warned that this area is currently changing as the whole marina is being redeveloped to create the new Al Bateen Wharf. Although being developed in phases, what's open one week may not be there the next.

O3

Sheikh Zayed
Grand Mosque

Location Al Maqta, Abu Dhabi **Web** szgmc.ae
Tel 02 419 1919 **Times** 9am-10pm (Saturday to Thursday),
closed Friday mornings
Price Guide Free **Map** 3 p.217

The stunning Sheikh Zayed Grand Mosque opened in 2007 and has captivated worshippers and visitors since. This work of art is the largest mosque in the UAE and one of the largest in the world, with a capacity for an astonishing 40,000 worshippers, which it often sees during Eid.

The Grand Mosque dominates arrival onto the island via the Al Maqta, Mussafah and Sheikh Zayed bridges, towering over the south of the island and so pristine and white that it appears to almost shimmer underneath the blue skies.

The mosque's first event was the funeral of its namesake, Sheikh Zayed, who is buried at the site.

Architecturally, the mosque was inspired by Mughal and Moorish traditions, with classical minarets. The most amazing features are perhaps the 80 domes, more than 1,000 columns, 24-carat gold chandeliers, or the world's largest hand-woven Persian carpet, which was designed by a renowned Iranian artist. If the effect is breathtaking during the day, then words can barely describe the vision that is the Grand Mosque illuminated at night.

Unlike other mosques, Sheikh Zayed Mosque is open for non-Muslims to tour between 9am and 10pm every day except for Friday mornings, although you might like to time your visit to coincide with one of the free 'walk in' guided tours that take place at 10am, 11am and 4.30pm during the week, at 4.30pm and 8pm on Friday, and at 10am, 11am, 2pm, 4.30pm and 8pm on Saturday. You will learn more about not only the mosque but Islam in general.

Remember to dress conservatively if you plan to visit the Grand Mosque. Men should avoid wearing shorts or short sleeves, while women should wear loose-fitting clothes that cover legs and arms. Shawls are provided at the entrance for ladies to cover their heads.

04
Al Meena Port

Location North-eastern tip of Abu Dhabi island
Map 4 p.224

The Al Meena port area is an excellent destination for visitors. Located on the north-eastern tip of the island, this is where you'll find Port Zayed, which is known for its working port, dhow harbour and souks.

This port is home to the fish, fruit and vegetable market, a carpet souk and the Iranian souk, which is an odd market-like collection of stores selling all sorts of bizarre knick-knacks. The Iranian traders come over on their dhows every three weeks or so – sometimes you'll be lucky and catch a new consignment of intricately-detailed pots and plates; other times there'll be no one around. These souks

offer an entirely different shopping experience to the malls: here, you can practise your bartering skills and walk away with a bargain.

The dhow harbour, off Port Road, is a contrast of past and present with several hundred dhows resting in their berths. Much like Al Bateen, it is a fascinating place to explore early in the morning when the fishermen return from sea. Try out the nearby restaurants, which offer an authentic selection of local cooking – grilled meats and seafood. The harbour is also worth a visit at sunset when the dhows return, particularly if you're a keen photographer.

Manarat Al Saadiyat

Location Saadiyat Island **Web** saadiyatculturaldistrict.ae
Tel 02 657 5800 **Times** 9am-8pm
Price Guide Free **Map** 5 p.225

There are, of course, huge amounts of excitement and enthusiasm for the cultural developments taking place on Saadiyat Island as completion dates draw nearer and nearer. Within a couple of years, visitors to the 'island of happiness' will be able to spend the morning in the Frank Gehry-designed Guggenheim Abu Dhabi, before spending a few hours in the Louvre Abu Dhabi (Jean Nouvel is the architect of that building), and finishing off the day in the Zayed National Museum, to be housed in an incredible Sir Norman Foster structure.

To find out more about the epic forthcoming cultural offerings of Saadiyat, including the Guggenheim Abu Dhabi, the Louvre Abu Dhabi, and the Zayed National Museum, head to Manarat Al Saadiyat. As well as being home to an interactive exhibition about the changing face of Saadiyat, it is also a cultural venue in its own right.

Manarat Al Saadiyat is part exhibition space and part Saadiyat visitor centre – a 15,400 square metre space where you'll find the Arts Abu Dhabi Gallery, the Contemporary Art Gallery and the Universal Art Gallery. A number of temporary exhibitions, showcasing works from some of the biggest names in modern art, have already passed through Manarat Al Saadiyat.

In addition, there are several galleries and auditoriums, as well as a 250-seat theatre and the excellent Fanr restaurant.

Women's Handicraft Centre

Location Karama St, Al Mushrif **Web** visitabudhabi.ae
Tel 02 447 6645 **Times** 7am-3pm (Sunday to Thursday)
Price Guide Dhs.5 per person **Map** 6 p.214

The Women's Handicraft Centre is a creative and artistic initiative to showcase local art, crafts and traditional practices. Sponsored by the Abu Dhabi Government and run by the Abu Dhabi Women's Association, the first point of call is the museum which, although on the small side, does provide some interesting examples of traditional local weaving, costume making and camel bags, along with some information on the crafts.

However, the small round huts at the back of the museum are what you really come here to see. Inside each, you'll find groups of Emirati women chatting and practising the traditional crafts of saddu, talli, textile weaving, embroidery, tailoring, basket-weaving, palm-tree frond weaving, and henna. These crafts have been practised by women and passed down through the generations; at the Women's Handicraft Centre, the women are continuing this proud tradition. Remember to remove your shoes before entering a hut and to ask permission before taking photos; and your pics should focus on the crafts rather than the women themselves. Male visitors should not get too close to the women.

Female visitors can experience the ancient art of henna, with a small hand design (that will last a couple of weeks) costing just Dhs.10. The onsite shop is also an excellent place to pick up some authentic keepsakes.

07

Folklore Gallery

Location Shk Zayed The First St, Al Khalidiyah **Web** folkloregallery.net
Tel 02 666 0361 **Times** 9am-10pm (Saturday to Thursday)
Price Guide Free **Map** 7 p.213

Abu Dhabi is setting itself up as the Middle East's art hub, and it's important to remember that, while giant mega-galleries are being constructed on Saadiyat Island there are also plenty of excellent small galleries already scattered throughout the city. The pick of the crop, arguably, is the Folklore Gallery, which has been open since 1995.

Ostensibly a framing gallery, it's still the best place to have artwork professionally framed or mounted. However, such is the passion for art, the gallery has become a lot more than that. The gallery showcases paintings, drawings and sculptures by its roster of resident artists. These items are all affordable entries into the world of art.

Abu Dhabi Art is a four-day event held every November at the UAE Pavilion on Saadiyat Island, showcasing work from 50 galleries in 20 countries. The Durub Al Tawaya programme also brings installations and performances to the capital.

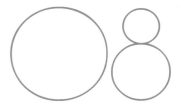

Al Maqtaa Fort

Location Nr Al Maqta Bridge, Al Maqta
Web visitabudhabi.ae
Map 8 p.217

This heavily renovated fort is one of the few remaining examples of its kind in Abu Dhabi city, and provides a wonderful contrast to the modern bridge right next to it. Your best view of Al Maqtaa Fort is likely to be on the approach to Abu Dhabi island, just before crossing one of the bridges.

Standing on the edge of the island, this 200-year-old fort is a reminder of times gone by, when its principal purpose was to protect Abu Dhabi from the bandits who prowled along the waterways.

Unfortunately, one of Abu Dhabi's most iconic and symbolic buildings cannot be directly accessed as it stands in a sensitive military zone and, therefore, remains closed to the public. Be careful when trying to photograph the fort as there are regular police patrols.

The Souk at Qaryat Al Beri

Location Qaryat Al Beri Complex, Al Maqta
Times 10am-10pm weekdays, 10am-11pm weekends,
3pm-11pm Fridays **Map** 9 p.217

The centre point of the Qaryat Al Beri complex – which lies between the Al Maqta and Mussafah bridges on the mainland, looking over the island and the Sheikh Zayed Grand Mosque – the Souk At Qaryat Al Beri is a contemporary adaptation of a typical souk.

Built over two levels, the complex is a fusion of age-old Arabian architecture with a Venetian theme, as romantic canals and lush gardens snake their way through the souk and connect it to the Shangri-La and Traders hotels.

The souk is a rabbit's warren of outlets, which are predominantly aimed at tourists and, as such, are maybe a little pricier than you'll find elsewhere. But, for the experience and atmosphere alone, the extra couple of dirhams are worth paying. The jewellery stands here are the best places to get your name written out in Arabic on a gorgeous necklace or pretty bracelet.

The real reason for the Souk at Qaryat Al Beri's increasing popularity, however, is its extensive and diverse collection of cafes, bars and restaurants. Almost all offer alfresco dining with views over the creek. Hop on one of the tourist dhows that sail the waterways for a different perspective of the souk.

10

Qasr Al Hosn

Location Markaziya West
Times 3pm-11pm during festival
Web visitabudhabi.ae **Map** 10 p.213

Wedged in between Old Airport Road, Al Nasr Street and Electra Street, just a few roads back from the Corniche, is exactly where you'll find Qasr Al Hosn. Often referred to as The Old Fort or The White Fort, whatever you call it, Qasr Al Hosn is the city's oldest surviving building, dating back to 1793. Surrounded on all four sides by towers, for decades, it was the official residence of the rulers of Abu Dhabi when they made the move from the Liwa Oasis to the island; from here, the sheikhs of Al Nahyan defended the island up until 1966. Its stunning fort and palace have since been beautifully restored, both inside and out. Today, lying in the heart of the capital, it is open to the public and is somewhere you can learn about the nation's important past and traditions.

Qasr Al Hosn is Abu Dhabi's main cultural attraction, representing the foundation of the country's capital and symbolising Emirati heritage. Visitors can enjoy this magnificent monument and learn about the nation's proud history and identity during its annual festival, when it is open to the public. Meanwhile, the neighbouring Cultural Foundation is open all year and has an amazing display of art, crafts as well as a library, theatre and exhibition spaces.

In recent years, Qasr Al Hosn has been lovingly restored and each February, the Fort and towers are temporarily opened to the public for an annual 10-day festival. Daily tours, events and spectacular shows are staged to promote Abu Dhabi's rich culture to the community.

GOT 'M' YET?

We could all do with a little "Mmmm" in our lives. Introducing
the 'M' card, Marina Mall Abu Dhabi new loyalty card that allows
our customers to earn points and redeem them instantly. To learn
more about the benefits and to sign-up, please visit the
Registration Desks at Marina Mall or **www.marinamall.ae**.

RFM
loyalty
LLC.

 /MarinaMallAbuD

 @MarinaMallAD

 @MarinaMallAD

Family Fun

Wadi Adventure

Family Fun
Introduction

Much of Abu Dhabi's appeal lies in the fact that it is truly a destination with something for everyone, and there are some stunning attractions that cater for the whole family.

Family plays a huge part in Abu Dhabi life, as well as being integral to Emirati culture and, no matter where you go, children are rarely expected to be seen and not heard. Many restaurants are abuzz with kids running around and there are numerous weekend brunches aimed specifically at families, with entertainment such as face painting, bouncy castles, art classes and games all laid on to help the younger family members enjoy the day every bit as much as mum and dad.

As well as some of the more individual family attractions listed in this chapter, the biggest malls in town provide bounteous destinations when it comes to keeping kids entertained. The majority have some sort of entertainment centre or games areas, such as Fun Works at Yas Mall, while others have extra special attractions, like the mini skating rink at Marina Mall and the splash park at Mushrif Mall. Cinemas also have a pretty open door policy, although you'd do well to respect the recommended age restrictions, as much out of consideration for other patrons as for the enjoyment of your children.

During the cooler months, Abu Dhabi's parks are great family locations, and you'll find everything from children's play areas with climbing frames, swings and slides to kiosks renting out bikes and pedal-powered go-karts, which are permanent fixtures at many of the largest parks. The beach parks along the Corniche are positively packed with activities to keep young ones entertained. And you'll likely find an ice cream stand or two to boot, of course, as well as other food stalls for grabbing a quick bite to eat.

If you're staying at one of Abu Dhabi's bigger resorts, the children may not ever want to leave the hotel, such is the range of activities available, from kids' clubs to swimming pools, and beaches to watersports. If your hotel doesn't have a kids' club, some locations, such as Saadiyat Beach Club, run children's clubs.

If your hotel doesn't have a pool, then, you chill out and have fun at the amazing waterpark on Yas Island. Hitting the beaches on the Corniche, or at Yas Marina are other great options for families. A word of caution while out and about by the beach; it is unwise to let your children swim in the sea unsupervised, especially at the public beaches, as there can sometimes be strong undercurrents.

Swimming pools outside of hotels are rare, making paying for a day pass at any of the larger resort hotels a fantastic way to spend the day. As well as access to the pool and facilities some hotels, such as Watercooled at the Hilton Abu Dhabi and Yas Marina offer watersports; such as banana boat riding, kayaking and stand-up-paddle boarding, all aimed at young kids.

Choosing Hotels

Check out what activities come included with your hotel booking before making a reservation. Some of the Yas Island hotels, for example, offer fantastic multi-activity packages that include family entry to Ferrari World and Yas Waterworld or even rounds of golf.

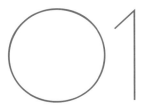

Emirates Park Zoo

Location Al Rahba **Web** emiratesparkzoo.com
Tel 02 501 0000 **Times** 9.30am-8pm (Sunday to Wednesday), 9am-9pm (Thursday to Saturday and Public Holidays) **Price Guide** Dhs.30 (adult), Dhs.20 (under 6), free (under 2) **Map** 1 p.211

The Emirates Park Zoo and Resort, which is a 30-minute drive or so outside of downtown Abu Dhabi, has recently seen some major renovations and is now one of the best and most popular kids' attractions in the emirate – although mum and day should enjoy visiting too.

The aim of the zoo is to give children the chance to get up close to their favourite animals, in order to combine learning about nature with touch and interaction. Wild attractions at the zoo include a bird park, a flamingo park, the 'Giraffe Cafe', an ocean park, the predator and primate sections, and the scary-sounding snake alley. There are, in total, more than 2,000 species on display, including camels, wallabies, pelicans, zebras, eels, clownfish, white tigers, brown bears, blue monkeys, chameleons and pythons. Anacondas, hippos and sea lions are on the way.

The highlight of a day at the Emirates Park Zoo has to be feeding the giraffes and zebras in the 'Giraffe Cafe', or bottlefeeding free-roaming lambs and goats in the children's farm area. Bunches of grass and carrots cost from Dhs.5.

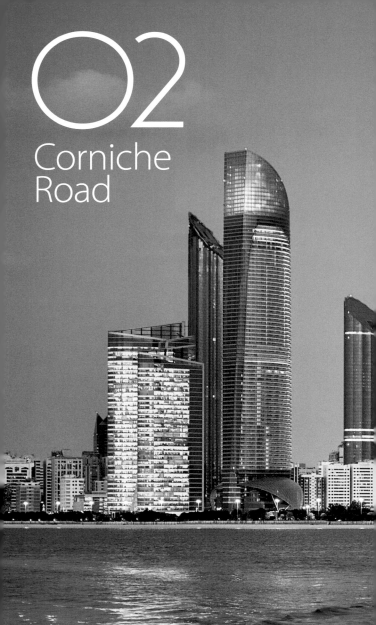

O2
Corniche
Road

Location Corniche Road, Abu Dhabi City
Map 2 p.213

Corniche Road boasts an impressive six kilometres of parks that include children's play areas, separate cycle and pedestrian paths, cafes and restaurants, and Corniche Beach, a series of life-guarded beachfronts.

There is the Family Park near King Khalid bin Abdul Aziz Street (26th Street), with its creative play areas for toddlers and older kids, a cafe, and BBQ and picnic areas; the Urban Park near Sheikh Rashid bin Saeed Al Maktoum Street, with its beautiful garden; the Lake Park near Muroor Street, known for its 'lake'; and the Formal Park by Baniyas Street, noted for its architecture and maze. There is plenty of parking on the city side of Corniche Road, and pedestrian underpasses at all the major intersections connect to the waterfront side.

These parks are very popular among city folk, especially during weekends, as families take a stroll, have picnics and get-togethers, or simply burn off some energy.

Bikes and pedal cars are for hire in the various parks and along the Corniche at reasonable rates. There are also plenty of places to grab snacks and drinks, while sporting and music events are regularly held in some of the public spaces.

Hili Fun City

Location Hili, Al Ain
Web hilifuncity.ae **Tel** 03 784 5542
Times Opening times vary
Price Dhs.50-60, free for kids
up to 89cm tall
Map 3 p.211

This 22-hectare, spacious and leafy park is the perfect out-of-town setting for family outings. There is a variety of arcade games and more than 30 attractions, ranging from gentle toddler rides, such as My First Car, Safari and the Hili Express train, to white-knuckle thrills for teens and adults, like Thunderbolt and the terrifying Sky Flyer.

The park has an amphitheatre where various singing, dancing and circus shows are put on throughout the day, should all the rides and rollercoasters leave you in need of something a little more sedate.

There are also plenty of grassy spaces for picnics and BBQs; visitors are welcome to arrive equipped with their own well-stocked picnic baskets that the whole family can enjoy under the shade of a tree while the little

Don't be fooled by Hili Fun City's tame exterior. Nothing prepares you for Sky Flyer, a white-knuckle ride where you hold on for dear life as you swing like a pendulum until you're upside down.

ones play on the lawns. If you forget a snack or two, don't worry as there are refreshment stands too.

The park is open 4pm to 10pm (Monday to Thursday), 12pm to 10pm (Friday and Saturday), with Wednesdays reserved for ladies and children only. The park is closed on Sundays and during Ramadan.

04

Abu Dhabi Falcon Hospital

Location Al Samkha **Web** falconhospital.com
Tel 02 575 5155 **Times** Tours at 10am and 2pm **Price Guide** Dhs.170
(adult), Dhs.60 (above 5); free (under 4) **Map** 4 p.211

The falcon is one of the great symbols of Arabia, initially revered for its hunting skills. Today, falconry is one of the proudest and most prestigious traditional sports practised throughout the Gulf. The tour at the Abu Dhabi Falcon Hospital is a fascinating insight into falcons, their importance in local culture, the history of falconry and the role of the falcon today.

The two-hour tour is genuinely interactive, and visitors have the chance to get up close and personal to falcons and falcon handlers, as well as see these magnificent birds in action.

Abu Dhabi Falcon Hospital originally opened in 1999 as a purely veterinary facility but has gone on to become one of the leading centres of its kind in the world, with a team of specialists providing diagnosis, treatment and disease prevention for falcons, other bird species and even poultry.

Also found on the same site is the Abu Dhabi Animal Shelter but, if you're an animal lover, you may want to give that a swerve, as a cute Saluki in need of adoption may mean you leave Abu Dhabi with a bigger souvenir than you'd planned!

05

Ferrari World

Location Yas Island West **Web** ferrariworldabudhabi.com
Tel 02 496 8001 **Times** 11am-8pm, open all week
Price Guide Dhs.205-250 **Map** 5 p.222

Part theme park, part simulator and part museum/learning centre for the legendary Italian brand, Ferrari World has won the hearts of UAE petrolheads and visitors alike. Out-and-out theme park fans should be impressed by the Formula Rossa – billed as the world's fastest rollercoaster, it reaches speeds of up to 240kmph. It's so fast riders have to wear safety goggles. The G-forces an F1 driver experiences are imitated by a 62-metre high ride that drops vertically through the park's roof, while a flume style water ride leads visitors through a series of twists, turns, rises and falls based on the workings of a Ferrari 599.

State-of-the-art simulators used to train Ferrari drivers give a realistic experience of being in the break-neck hustle and bustle of a real grand prix, while young wannabe Hamiltons and Alonsos can attend a drivers' school. And anyone who has ever wanted, well, just about anything adorned with the famous 'prancing horse' logo, won't go home disappointed after a visit to the store.

If thrills and spills aren't your thing, then visit Bell'Italia for an aerial tour of a miniature Italy. Also, all manner of traditional Italian foods and flavours are on offer, but you should try Cipriani Yas Island if you're feeling flash.

Al Ain Zoo

Location Zoo District, Al Ain **Web** alainzoo.ae **Tel** 03 799 2000 **Times** Various, open daily **Price Guide** Dhs.20 (adults), Dhs.10 (3 to 12), free (under 3) **Map** 6 p.211

Stretching over 900 hectares, this is the largest and best zoo in the region. With ample greenery, a casual stroll through the paths that criss-cross the park makes for a wonderful family day out. As well as seeing apes, reptiles and big cats, you can get up close to local species such as the Arabian oryx and sand gazelle, or pay a visit to the fantastic birdhouse.

The zoo is a centre for endangered species conservation and visitors can look forward to spotting true rarities. Nearly 30% of the 180 species are endangered and the park is even home to a stunning pair of white tigers and white lions. Family nights with fun activities take place on Wednesdays. A park train regularly departs from the central concourse, providing a whirlwind tour. Given its sprawling size, the easiest way to explore the zoo is to purchase the service of a buggy and driver when you buy your tickets. It's best to get there early to enjoy the cooler temperatures and quieter crowds.

Children and adults alike are sure to be delighted by a trip to the giraffe feeding station where you can purchase a cup of carrots for Dhs.30 and use it to feed these fun, long-necked creatures by hand.

07

Yas Waterworld

Location Yas Island West **Web** yaswaterworld.com
Tel 02 414 2000 **Times** Opens at 10am, closing times vary
Price Guide Dhs.195-440 **Map** 7 p.222

Yas Waterworld burst on to the scene in 2012 achieving the seemingly impossible – in a country that boasts some of the best waterparks that can be found anywhere in the world, it managed to raise the bar even higher. The large park is based on an ancient Arabian tale involving the search for a lost pearl, and it draws on this to combine touches of the traditional (architecture and souk-style shopping) with the very latest in water entertainment and technology. There are 43 rides, slides and attractions in total. As well as cafes, waterplay zones for toddlers, exciting kids' pools, a long lazy river and an interactive pearl diving attraction, the park has some incredible white-knuckle fun, such as the world's first rattling water slide.

The Aqualoop spins riders 360 degrees around in a loop, while the Water Bomber roller-coaster is the region's first suspended and longest ride, reaching speeds of up to 55kmph; there's also a six-person tornado ride.

Wadi Adventure

Location Jebel Hafeet, Al Ain **Web** wadiadventure.ae
Tel 03 781 8422 **Times** 11am-8pm (weekdays), 10am-8pm (weekends)
Price Guide Dhs.25-Dhs.100+ **Map** **8** p.221

Wadi Adventure is the first facility of its kind anywhere in the Middle East.

Perhaps the best way to think of Wadi Adventure is as a waterpark with a difference; instead of slides and rides, here you'll find three world-class white water rafting and kayaking runs, totalling more than a kilometre in length. Whether you choose to get stuck in with a rafting session or take a one-on-one kayak session, there are enough options to suit your needs and past experiences. A giant conveyor belt drags you to the summit of the rapids and then it's up to you to complete the course. The beginner rapids are suitable for families (kids have to be taller than 1.2 metres). Don't be surprised if you capsize on the tougher rapids; just make sure you listen carefully to the safety instructions.

If water isn't your thing, then the tree-top obstacles and canyon swings should keep you occupied. There are also a few food and drink outlets for refuelling.

Surfer dudes can also get in on the action with a huge surf pool that generates a three-metre high wave every 90 seconds; while the more experienced surfers tackle the big waves at the back of the pool, beginners can take lessons nearer the shore.

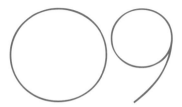

Zayed Sports City

Location Al Madina Al Riyadiya **Web** zsc.ae
Tel 02 403 4200 **Times** Open all week **Price Guide** Varies
Map 9 p.216

Zayed Sports City is a sports and entertainment destination with more than 30 sporting activities for the whole family. It has an Olympic and standard ice rink, a large outdoor park, paintballing for all ages and a new golf simulator. The complex also has a nine-court tennis centre, with lessons available. Each January, they host the Mubadala World Tennis Championship and community tournaments run throughout the year.

The Khalifa International Bowling Centre has a whopping 40 lanes, video games and some fantastic restaurants, such as Chinese favourite, Noodle Ball. The centrepiece of Zayed Sports City is the UAE's largest stadium, holding major international sporting events throughout the year, such as the UAE football finals. Visiting premier football teams, from the UK, also make an appearance regularly.

English Premier League team Manchester City, which of course has strong links to Abu Dhabi, has a football school based at Zayed Sports City, where City's top coaches and players often take part in training sessions.

Al Forsan

Location Khalifa City **Web** alforsan.com **Tel** 02 556 8555
Times Varies **Price Guide** Dhs.55 with Dhs.25 credit
Map 10 p.219

From the entrance, Al Forsan International Sports Resort looks no different to any other five-star resort but, as you walk through the grounds, you'll uncover its amazing assets.

Firstly, there are two large cable parks. One of the lakes at Al Forsan is dedicated to beginner boarders. Over on the expert lake, wakeboarders and wakeskaters zip their way around the outside of the lake, jumping over ramps while practising surface switches and superhuman tricks.

Al Forsan also offers some incredible paintballing fields, as well as clay pigeon shooting, archery and horse riding. The motorsports centre offers up a range of petrol-powered activities. There's a 1.2km CIK-approved circuit and vehicles with top speeds of up to 120kmph available (for experienced karters); there's also a kids' karting track. The dual circuit, fully-floodlit, off-road buggy track allows two buggies to race without any chance of collision.

If you've ever dreamed of becoming a daredevil stunt driver, there's an alternative circuit at Al Forsan where you can learn the arts of drifting, skid controls and power turns.

Showstopper Restaurants

Fairmont Bab Al Bahr

Showstopper
Restaurants
Introduction

Abu Dhabi's gastronomic landscape is a tasty battleground with celebrity chefs competing against bargain ethnic eateries to win your hard-earned cash.

Variety is the spice of life where Abu Dhabi's restaurant scene is concerned, with all the nationalities that now call this city home bringing their own particular specialities and flavours to bear on local gastronomy. You will truly find everything from molecular gastronomy to Mexican-inspired pub grub and back-street curry houses, and they're all equally delicious.

Many of Abu Dhabi's most beloved restaurants are located within hotels and leisure clubs, and their popularity is partly due to the fact that these are virtually the only outlets where you can drink alcohol with your meal. Almost all other restaurants are unlicensed. There's quite a hefty mark-up on drinks, with a decent bottle of wine often costing as much as your meal. The city has some superb independent restaurants and cafes that shouldn't be ignored just because they don't serve booze. Some are ethnic eateries lining the streets of Abu Dhabi's oldest areas, or fresh food cafes in the big malls.

However, as much as there are cheap eats and reasonable offers, Abu Dhabi is best known for its over-the-top lavishness and this applies to its restaurants as much as everything else. Big name celebrity chefs rub shoulders with Michelin-starred culinary giants in Abu Dhabi; Marco Pierre White helms a couple of restaurants at the Fairmont Bab Al Bahr, celeb Emirati chef Ali Salem Edbowa is head chef at Emirates Palace's Mezlai, and Gary Rhodes has opened the acclaimed Rhodes 44 at the St Regis Saadiyat Island Resort. These names alone speak volumes about the sheer variety of high-end food in the city, while plenty of other top-class eateries that may not (yet!) boast a famous chef or name are forging their own reputations through quality and fantastic creativity.

Meanwhile, uber-brands such as Hakkasan at Emirates Palace and the iconic Japanese, Zuma at The Galleria on Al Maryah Island have appeared in recent years, including BOA Steakhouse at Eastern Mangroves Promenade, The Collection's fine-diner, Koi, and Yas Island's Fanr Restaurant and Cipirani.

Ramadan Dining

During Ramadan, opening and closing times of restaurants change considerably. Because eating and drinking in public is forbidden during daylight hours, many places only open after sunset then keep going well into the early hours. The breaking of the fast (iftar) is popular with both fasting Muslims and non-fasting expats keen to try the traditional local delicacies. The practice of suhoor (think of it as the midnight feast that sustains Muslims through the following day's fast) has also become a more communal event that people of all religious backgrounds take part in during Ramadan.

Fishmarket

Location InterContinental Abu Dhabi
Web dining-intercontinental-ad.ae **Tel** 02 666 6888
Times 12.30pm-4pm and 7pm-11pm **Map** 1 p.212

If you're a seafood fan, then the chances are that Fishmarket will quickly be added to your list of favourites once you've scoffed down some of the catches of the day that are served up at this marina-side venue.

The concept is simplicity itself. Guests are confronted by an extensive array of fresh seafood, along with a cartload of fresh vegetables, and a range of noodle and rice varieties. Take a look, see what tickles your fancy, and then opt for a fish, the style of cooking (grilled, sautéed or fried) and let the chef know what kind of sauce (green curry, red curry or oyster sauce) and accompaniments most float your boat.

Portions tend to err on the side of gargantuan, but the flavours are sensational and the fish is as fresh as it gets. The shack-style, tropical island decor and the always smiley service make Fishmarket feel a long way from Abu Dhabi, and it's an easy place to relax and have fun. A word of warning: the menu concentrates almost solely on seafood with few choices for carnivores and vegetarians.

The rope-bound bamboo pillars, sailor-blue tablecloths and lobster-filled fish tanks give Fishmarket a rustic seaside shack feel – the perfect setting to enjoy fresh grilled red snapper, jumbo prawns or fresh, local hammour.

02

Pachaylen

Location Eastern Mangroves Hotel & Spa by Anantara
Web abudhabi.anantara.com **Tel** 02 656 1000
Times 7pm-11pm **Map** **2** p.215

If the rest of Eastern Mangroves is a delicate balance between the Arabian and the Far Eastern, then its signature restaurant, Pachaylen, is a full-on embrace of Anantara's Thai heritage. From the all-Thai kitchen and waiting-on staff to the menu and the aromas pouring out from the open kitchen, it's authentic but sophisticated South East Asian through and through.

You'll be hard-pressed to find a more beautifully decked-out restaurant in Abu Dhabi and, if you're going to be picking up the tab, make sure you sit at the golden chair – there's one at each table and it's your right as the host!

You'll be equally hard-pressed to uncover a tastier, lovelier welcome than the traditional miang kham street snack that's served up as an amuse-bouche. After that, it's traditional Thai done in the tastiest way you'll find anywhere outside of Bangkok. The soft shell crab salad is the standout starter, while you should look no further than the slow-cooked Thai curries for your main course. It is all a long way from traditional street food, and the spiciness isn't overdone.

Pachaylen delivers again on dessert; the banana pancake spring rolls or sticky rice and fruit are the perfect ways to finish.

Ray's Grill

Location Jumeirah At Etihad Towers
Web jumeirah.com **Tel** 02 811 5666 **Times** 12pm-3.30pm (Sunday to Thursday) and 7pm-11:30pm (Sunday to Friday) **Map** 3 p.212

Abu Dhabi is jam-packed with very good restaurants but discovering a world-class steakhouse is definitely worth savouring. That's the niche that Ray's Grill fills. Inside, the restaurant is striking too, with elegant tables spread around an open kitchen and incredible views from its 63rd floor vantage point.

As Abu Dhabi sparkles below, it's the service – just about perfect – and the food that will really hold your attention. For appetizers, sample fresh oysters, cured salmon and pan seared scallops. For mains, the restaurant lives up to its name with an imaginative selection of signature grills and prime beef cuts sourced from some of the finest cattle producers in Ireland, United States and Australia. Succulent beef is dry aged for a minimum of 28 days and their unique char grill uses real charcoal and is kept at 375-400°c to create a distinct flavour. The result is tenderised steak and other grilled meats to a standard not easily found. Add to this one of their mouthwatering sauces (saffron cream or salsa verde?) before completing your dish with a tasty side order.

For pre-or post- dinner drinks, Ray's Bar, a floor below, is delightful and will round off any evening in style and elegant surroundings.

O4

Nolu's

Locations Al Bandar, Al Raha
Tel 02 557 9500
Times Open daily, 8pm-11pm
Map 4 p.220

Nolu's Afghani food served in a contemporary California-inspired ambience typifies the cultural blend that makes Abu Dhabi's restaurants so unique. Located in the sleek new Al Bandar housing development, Nolu's has quickly established itself on the capital's restaurant scene, particularly due to its popularity among members of the royal family.

The Afghani dishes on the menu are mostly limited to appetisers; the delicious mantoo, beef and onion dumplings, are a particularly mouth-watering choice. The remainder of the menu is comprised of pasta, burgers, and sandwiches.

Nolu's features some of the healthiest meals in the capital and,

in contrast to other places, it's easy to find vegetarian and gluten-free options with fresh ingredients. Their salads in particular show the California influence of the owner-chef, with locally-sourced and unusual ingredients. The limited dessert offerings include a delectable American-style cheesecake.

The earth-tone decor, light-filled rooms, and views of the water add to the chilled-out vibe, and the attentive staff is happy to let eaters linger long after the plates have been cleared. Nolu's is quite the hidden gem.

> While you're in Al Bandar, take a walk along the marina for a unique vantage point of the Yas Island attractions, located just across the water.

Graciously Thai
in the Heart of
Abu Dhabi

For more information, please call +971 2 698 8888
or email reservations.abudhabi@dusit.com
www.Dusit.com

05

Al Mayass

Location Sheraton Abu Dhabi Hotel & Resort **Web** almayass.com
Tel 02 644 0440 **Times** 12pm-11:30pm **Map** 5 p.214

Lebanese restaurants in Abu Dhabi are as common as palm trees, so the fact that Al Mayass is packed on a nightly basis says a lot about the quality of its food. The menu has an interesting mixture of Lebanese and Armenian dishes and a range of both hot and cold mezze, or appetizers, as well as the usual entrees and salads.

The food is served in a cosy, family-friendly environment that lends itself to business meetings as well as dinners out with friends. Shisha pipes are available and the lingering smoke makes for even more of a Middle Eastern experience; if it's not your thing, however, ask to be seated on the terrace.

Meal-wise, the cherry beef kebab is an absolute standout, with a mouthwatering sweet and tangy sauce. Several variations kick up the classic hummus, while the knafeh and orange blossom tea make for a perfect ending to one of Abu Dhabi's best Lebanese meals. Delightful desserts such as mint sorbet, nutty baklava or creamy lemon curd are hard to pick.

The stalwart Sheraton is also home to other time-tested favourites such as the Mexican El Sombrero and Italian La Mamma.

Safina

Location Saadiyat Beach Club **Web** saadiyatbeachclub.ae
Tel 02 656 3555 **Times** 12pm-3pm (Saturday to Thursday), 6pm-10pm
(Saturday to Wednesday), 6pm-11pm (Thursday to Friday) **Map** 6 p.225

Located in the beautiful surroundings of the ultra hip Saadiyat Beach Club, with a terraced area that reaches towards the giant pool, Safina is a genuinely top class offering. The Mediterranean restaurant has an airily elegant feel to it, with the large open kitchen serving as the centrepiece. If the weather is agreeable – and it usually is – then pick a table out on the terrace and soak up the ambiance.

The menu reflects the fresh, airy ambience of both the beach club and the restaurant; even heartier fare such as braised wagyu ravioli, risotto and the assortment of steaks are treated with a lightness of touch, while the plentiful use of salads and fresh seasonings leave you feeling healthy and full.

The delicate flavours in dishes like the burrata cheese, the wild mushroom veloute, or the pepper crusted yellowfin tuna suggest confident and creative hands at work in the open kitchen. If you're lucky enough to dine on one of the occasional jazz nights, the sweet sounds of jazz at sunset will be the perfect background to your meal.

07

Marco Pierre White Steakhouse and Grill

Does a beautifully appointed restaurant with exact yet friendly service, delivering British comfort food elevated to superb standards, sound like your idea of heaven? Then get to Marco Pierre White Steakhouse and Grill immediately.

A single bite of the foie gras starter tells you that Marco has brought all his experience to bear in his Abu Dhabi restaurant. And, while the flame-lit venue may look beautiful, it is anything but style over substance.

The menu is enough to give vegetarians nightmares – great cuts of meat take top billing here, alongside the superb wine list – but, even amongst some pretty stiff competition, it's the steaks that stand out. Tuck into a pepper sauce-topped fillet and you'll know why. The sumptuous surroundings will have you spending the whole night wallowing in this fine-dining, wine-fuelled experience.

The set menu with wine pairings is nothing short of exquisite: Scottish smoked salmon with slow poached quail egg; crab veloute with Alaskan king crab tortie; slow roasted Wagyu tenderloin; and Eton mess to finish – perfection on a plate.

Top 10 Family Venues

Dine Map 11 p.216
Aloft Abu Dhabi – 02 654 5121
Mondo Map 12 p.214
Abu Dhabi Country Club – 02 657 7785
Noodle House Map 13 p.217
Souk at Qaryat Al Beri – 02 558 1699
Choices Brunch Map 14 p.222
Yas Island Rotana – 02 656 4000
Carluccio's Map 15 p.214
The Galleria Mall – 02 677 1261
La Mamma Map 16 p.214
Sheraton Abu Dhabi – 02 697 0224
Jones The Grocer Map 17 p.214
Al Wahdah – 02 443 8762
Zest Map 18 p.211
Al Ain Rotana – 03 754 5111
Shakespeare and Co. Map 19 p.213
WTC Souk – 02 639 9626
Stars 'n' Bars Map 20 p.222
Yas Marina & Yacht Club – 02 565 0101

If you fancy a more casual affair, pop next door to Frankie's, a bustling Italian managed by jockey Frankie Dettori and MPW himself.

08

Ushna

Location The Souk at Qaryat Al Beri **Tel** 02 558 1769
Times 12.30pm-11.30pm (weekdays), 12.30pm-12.30am (weekends)
Map 8 p.217

Another of the venues that is making the Souk at Qaryat Al Beri the gastronomic epicentre of Abu Dhabi, Ushna is an Indian restaurant – but not as you know it. It is Indian cuisine filtered through a prism of high-end dining, and Ushna's sophisticated surroundings perfectly complement the beautifully prepared food.

Punjabi classics like lamb pasanda, aloo tikki ragda, tandoori murgh and paneer are all delicately flavoured and never over-spiced, allowing the quality of the produce to shine. The curries are, of course, sensational, and side orders like aloo jeera, dal and rice are just as good. If you have room, the freshly-prepared breads are almost meals in their own right and well worth sharing.

The service mirrors the superb setting and there's a good selection of premium grape and cocktails to choose from. During the cooler months, bag a table by the water overlooking the Grand Mosque for a romantic night out.

> Vegetarian dishes include tandoori sabzi – glazed mixed vegetables marinated in vinegar and spices and cooked in a clay oven; or gobhi ke sabzi – an excellent Indian homemade delicacy of fresh cauliflower with ginger and tomatoes.

Benjarong

Location Dusit Thani, Abu Dhabi **Web** dusit.com **Tel** 02 698 8888
Times 2.30pm-11.30pm (daily) **Map** 9 p.214

Thai fare from a Thai-owned chain that lives up to expectations. Located in the elegant Dusit Thani, the welcoming restaurant oozes elegance as well. If you know what you love and love what you know, it's easy to choose the rice, noodles and pad Thai, which are all present. Benjarong is particularly recommended for these classic Thai staples; the Pad Thai is perfect and beautifully presented, while the King Prawn Tom Yum is decidedly yummy. The tantalising menu tempts you with its standard Thai green or curries too, but tempts you again to try its more unusual and exotic dishes.

For something a bit different, you can 'create your own curry' and the attentive staff will try hard to ascertain exactly how spicy you like it. A good venue for a lingering romantic meal which pulls on your heart strings rather than your purse strings.

Benjarong delivers on every level and is a real winner for authentic Thai.

For fine dining and variety in the capital, the Dusit Thani's Capital Grill is another excellent option. It doesn't come cheap, but the Wagyu beef cuts and sauces are simply mouth-watering. This delightful steakhouse is irresistible and scores highly for meat-lovers everywhere.

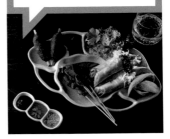

10

Mezlai

Location Emirates Palace **Web** kempinski.com
Tel 02 690 7999 **Times** 1pm-10.30pm (Monday to Sunday)
Map 10 p.212

Mezlai is a fairly unique offering. For starters, it has a celebrity head chef that very few guests will have heard of – Ali Salem Edbowa is a regular on local TV stations and is one of a handful of skilful kitchen maestros who are helping to raise the art and profile of Gulf cuisine.

Mezlai means 'the old lock of the door', which aptly reflects its ability to unlock the secrets of authentic Emirati cuisine to both a local and international audience. As befits an establishment that prides itself on being the UAE's first Emirati restaurant, Mezlai's Arabic-themed decor features plenty of intricate and well thought out design touches, such as majlis corners and memorabilia from the country's early days. The stained glass lanterns may be traditional but they also serve to cast an atmospheric spell over proceedings.

In terms of ingredients, you'll find few surprises; the food relies on traditional staples like rice, meat and fish. But dishes are prepared with a sprinkling of regional influences from across the Middle East. True to the UAE's culinary traditions, there's an emphasis on seafood and you'll sample specialities like Weld Al Walad – shark soup – and grilled Gulf hammour, while carnivores are treated to camel meat and lamb medfoun.

Mezlai is not the only culinary gem at the Emirates Palace. Be sure to explore the dining delights at chic seafood brasserie Sayad (the Arabic word for 'fisherman') and the award-winning, authentic Italian eatery Mezzaluna.

only few things age better with time...

GMP

www.graymackenzie.com

Best Bars

Bars

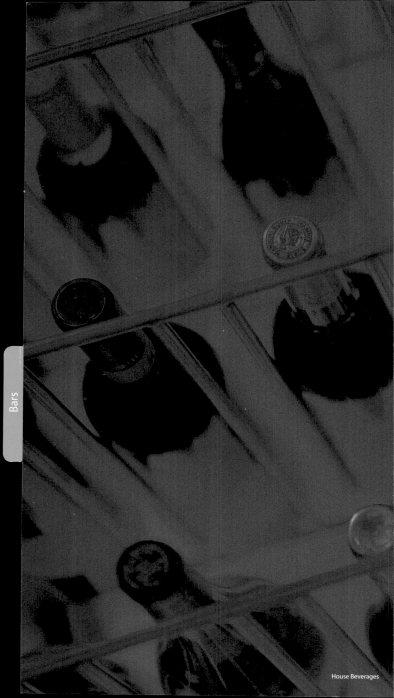

Bars

Best Bars
Introduction

The days when Abu Dhabi's bar scene was little more than a sandy backwater are long gone; what you'll find today is an eclectic and exciting nightlife.

Standards are high in Abu Dhabi, due to the particular demands of the city's utterly unique and multicultural drinking crowd. The city's community is such an eclectic mix of creeds and kinds that there's an incredibly varied range of drink and bar expectations. So, have these expectations been met? Indeed, they have – Abu Dhabi has responded to the challenge by 'raising the bars' to create a parade of interesting and atmospheric venues vying to meet every drinker's desire.

From the downright dirty (but fun) dive bars of downtown to some of the world's most glamorous and renowned celebrity party venues, Abu Dhabi has it all, with every bar attempting to stand out among the city's five-star fleet. Maybe you're in a boardies and flip-flops mood and after a laidback sundowner? Or perhaps you're looking to throw on your swankiest threads and take to the town for a raucous night that you'll never remember? The city bows to your every request.

Although, due to the taxes levied on alcohol, drinking in Abu Dhabi can be fairly costly, the city is also bulging with inventive promotions and theme nights that allow you to get merry without paying over the odds. The fairer sex, in particular, can paint the town red without spending a fil thanks to the whole host of drink-specific ladies nights that take place during the week – usually on Monday, Tuesday or Wednesday.

When it comes to bar itineraries, Abu Dhabi can offer a more varied night out than many other cities, since punters are able to hop into a taxi and zoom between bar stools at opposite sides of the city quickly and cheaply.

The venues listed in this chapter highlight the various types of bars in Abu Dhabi, both in terms of style and location. Obviously, personal preference plays a significant part in such a list, so keep in mind that these were chosen to emphasise the different varieties in the city; there's not just one bar with great views, one place for sundowners or one beach bar to hit for laid-back cocktails – these are just some of the best and most popular haunts.

So, whether you're looking for that quirky one-of-a-kind bar, a suave cigar lounge or a sticky floored dingy dive club, Abu Dhabi has it all. And, if it doesn't exist right now, it probably will next week!

Door Policy

Certain bars and nightclubs have a selective entry policy. Sometimes 'membership' is introduced to control the clientele, but it is often only enforced during busy periods or to disallow entry for certain groups. Large groups (especially those consisting of all males) and singles, for example, may be turned away from busier bars and clubs without much of an explanation. Avoid the inconvenience by breaking the group up or by going in a mixed-gender group. Some of the city's most popular hotspots can be nearly impossible to enter on certain nights unless you're on the guest list, so be sure to call and book in advance.

Skylite

Location Yas Viceroy
Web viceroyhotelsandresorts.com
Tel 02 656 0600 **Times** 6pm-1am
(daily), 4pm-1am (Friday)
Map 1 p.222

Rush, another bar at Yas Viceroy, is located in the bridge that straddles the race track. Saturdays' R&B nights bring a big crowd ready to get down to classic and contemporary music.

When you head out in Abu Dhabi for the first time, you want to go somewhere super-stylish that makes a statement, and venues don't come much swankier than Skylite. Perched on the roof of the iconic Yas Viceroy hotel, the stunning views from this rooftop lounge bar will blow you away, and even the most style conscious will appreciate the modern, imaginative decor. After all, if it's a good enough bar for the Grand Prix's Hollywood A-listers to come and party…

There are light bites and long wine, champagne and cocktail lists to choose from, while the dress code errs on the smarter and trendier side of casual. The best time to enjoy Skylite is as the sun goes down, but it's easy enough to spend all night here too.

O2

Sho Cho

Location The Souk at Qaryat Al Beri **Web** sho-cho.com
Tel 02 558 1117 **Times** 12-3.30pm and 6pm-2.45am
(Sunday to Thursday), 12-2.45am (Friday and Saturday)
Map 2 p.217

For a while now, Sho Cho's fun brand of sushi and cocktails teamed with modern Japanese style had made it one of Dubai's most achingly hip restaurants and nightspots, so the residents of Abu Dhabi were overjoyed to find that Sho Cho had successfully made the leap to the capital. All the same elements have been retained – the interiors are a real delight, while the decking area boasts the incredible creekside views that are almost par for the course at Qaryat Al Beri.

The cuisine is perhaps best described as oriental fusion, with plenty of fish and sushi dishes on the menu, including maki rolls, tempura, sashimi, salads and appetisers such as soft shell crab spring roll and king fish ceviche. The brunches (Friday lunchtime and Sunday evening) are extremely popular, but describing Sho Cho as a restaurant is misleading given that it has fast become a favourite among Abu Dhabi's party-loving socialites.

Guest DJs and live bands are regularly brought in to provide the soundtracks, with Wednesday's ladies' night (two free vodka martinis) one of the most popular in the city.

The Beachcomber

Location Sheraton Abu Dhabi Hotel & Resort
Web sheratonabudhabihotel.com
Tel 02 677 3333 **Times** 4pm-1am (daily)
Map 3 p.214

With Abu Dhabi's reputation for A-list venues, you'd be forgiven for thinking that all its bars are simply places for the beautiful people to be seen. But there are plenty of alternatives on offer too and, if your idea of a good bar is a little more relaxed, then head for The Beachcomber.

Sat between the pool and the private lagoon at Sheraton Abu Dhabi, this chilled-out beach bar feels more Caribbean than Arabian, which makes it popular with after-work and weekend crowds, as well as holidaymakers. It serves up a tapas menu that, while not authentically Spanish, does provide the ideal accompaniment to the cocktails that are on offer.

04

Jazz Bar & Dining

Location Hilton Abu Dhabi **Web** hilton.com **Tel** 02 681 1900
Times 7pm-12.30am (Saturday-Wednesday); 7pm-1.30am
(Thursday and Friday) **Map** 4 p.212

The name of this venerable institution is a slight misnomer. The house band doesn't play jazz, but rather covers of flashback and contemporary danceable music. And the dining, while more than adequate, is not the biggest reason to keep coming back. That honour goes to the atmosphere, which is lively every single night of the week.

Housed in one of Abu Dhabi's oldest hotels, the Jazz Bar, as it's more commonly known, has had plenty of time to build a reputation for fun. It attracts a slightly older crowd than most other bars in the capital, but that's certainly not to say that it's any less fun. People are dancing in the aisles between the tables, and the Monday ladies' nights (free red, white, and bubbly for the fairer sex) are particularly popular.

The menu has a decent selection of continental soups, sandwiches, and mains. Dinner guests are advised to arrive early, as carrying on a conversation can be a challenge once the band gets started. But given the infectious energy of the band, you'll probably be singing along.

Sip on perfectly mixed cocktails as the sun sets over a luxurious oasis in the midst of the mystic Liwa desert.

Suhail at Qasr Al Sarab Desert Resort by Anantara

Lemon & Lime

Location The Westin Abu Dhabi Golf Resort & Spa, Khalifa City
Web westinabudhabigolfresort.com **Tel** 02 616 9999
Times 5pm-1am (daily) **Map** 5 p.218

Lemon & Lime is a venue tailor-made for epicureans who prefer their nights to be focused on quality rather than decibels. This extremely elegant wine and cigar bar is the kind of place where you can get together to start your night, or simply spend the whole evening soaking up the chic atmosphere. Its off-island location means it is usually busy rather than jam-packed, which perfectly suits the laid-back sophistication of the venue.

The decor is contemporary luxury, although the amazing golf course views dominate. There's an excellent pianist who tinkles the ivories seductively earlier in the evening, and ramps it up as the night gets going.

The variety of wines on offer is exceptional. Fans of fine vintages should keep their eye out for the regular wine and champagne offers, and the one-off special events, which provide real value for money.

O1NE

Location Yas Island, Nr Yas Tunnel **Web** o1neyasisland.com
Tel 052 788 8111 **Times** Thursday and Friday, 11pm-4am
Map 6 p.222

O1NE is unlike anything else in the city: a proper megaclub that is on par with what you'd find in Dubai, Las Vegas, or even Ibiza. The graffiti-lined exterior gives a taste of the over-the-top opulence that lies inside. That lavishness includes 350 sq m of projection screens, extensive VIP areas, and a catwalk down the centre of the club. The screens show images from trendy global cities, so one night you may be in Singapore, the next, Rio. A night out at O1NE doesn't start early and doesn't come cheap: a place this popular has no need for promotions or incentives. Book a table ahead and don't bother showing up until well after midnight when the place really gets into full swing.

The resident mixers spin mainly house, but regular guest DJ appearances vary up the offerings.

O1NE is operated by Sky Management, known for SKYBAR Beirut as well as the Formula One after parties. In the past, they've booked Missy Elliot, David Guetta, Prince, 50 Cent, and Ludacris, so O1NE will surely follow in this star-studded vein.

07

P&C by Sergi Arola

Location Shangri-La Hotel Qaryat Al Beri
Web shangri-la.com **Tel** 02 509 8777
Times 7pm-11.30pm (Sunday to Thursday),
1pm-4pm and 8pm-11.30pm (Friday)
Map 7 p.217

Inside this popular venue is a sleek monochrome world of black, white and silver, representing the decadent duo of caviar and pearls. There are silver bead curtains, black and white mosaic floors, black walls and ceilings, and large picture windows through which twinkling lights illuminate the black night sky like precious stones. Recessed lighting and the dark theme make it a low-light setting, while seating is arranged on comfortable banquettes. P&C by Sergi Arola is where you can enjoy Mediterranean-Levantine culinary treats washed down with great wines and cocktails.

The airy rooftop lounge is one of the trendiest and most beautiful terrace bars you're likely to find anywhere in the world. Here, cocktails and tapas are served against the backdrop of the white marble of Sheikh Zayed Grand Mosque.

As you might expect, three types of caviar are on offer: Beluga, Sevruga and Oscietra. Prices and service reflect the luxury and, while dinner for two will set you back around Dhs.1,200, this has not dimmed the venue's popularity.

La Cava

Location Rosewood Abu Dhabi **Web** rosewoodhotels.com
Tel 02 813 5550 **Times** 5pm-1am (daily) **Map** **8** p.214

Descending the wooden spiral staircase into La Cava is like travelling into a hidden chamber. The stone walls, concrete floors, and wooden shelves full of bottles give the wine bar an austere, elegant feel. It's unlike anything else in the city and, once you've entered, it's easy to lose sight of the fact that you're in Abu Dhabi and not an old European capital.

The speciality of a wine bar, naturally, is wine, and La Cava boasts an impressive collection of over 1,000 labels with a total of 8,500 bottles ready to serve at any time. The menu includes reds, white, and champagnes from the usual suspects of France, Spain, Italy, South Africa and the Americas with a few welcome surprises like India, Austria, and Hungary also included.

The sommeliers are friendly but unobtrusive and very knowledgeable about the range of labels on offer. Unusually tasty bar snacks are served alongside the wine, although a delicious range of tapas are available for those seeking something a little more substantial.

The bar is nonsmoking, a rarity in Abu Dhabi, although a separate smoking room exists for those who wish to order from the cigar menu. Tapas and wine tasting promotions change monthly, so it's worth a call to inquire about the latest offers.

09

Coopers Bar & Restaurant

Location Park Rotana **Web** rotana.com
Tel 02 657 3333 **Times** 12pm until 2.30am (weekdays) and 4am
(weekends) **Map** 9 p.217

Located in the Park Rotana, Coopers is a popular pub with good service and solid food. Its reputation is built on consistency – the drinks will be strong, the service will be quick, the food will be plentiful, and the music will be loud. They screen major sporting events, and on game days, tables are filled with groups of mates focused on the match. Regular happy hours and ladies' nights also help to bring in the crowds.

Expats throng the reasonably-priced Friday brunch to enjoy a family-friendly atmosphere and decent pub food. The scene starts to get less tame around sundown, and late at night it can turn into quite a raucous affair, with a DJ playing very danceable music and the crowds taking full advantage to show off their moves.

The outside terrace overlooking the pool offers comfortable seating and a chance to escape the often-smoky interior. If you plan to eat, it's best to call ahead and make a table reservation; otherwise you might spend the night standing.

10

Relax@12

Location Aloft Abu Dhabi **Web** relaxat12.com
Tel 02 654 5183 **Times** 5pm-2am (Saturday, Sunday, Monday and Wednesday) and 5pm-3am (Tuesday, Thursday and Friday)
Map 10 p.216

If rooftop cocktails, heady views and a spot of sushi sound like your idea of bliss – and, let's face it, why wouldn't they? – then you're going to love spending time at Relax@12.

This isn't some high-octane nightspot; the name says it all – chill out in the sleek lounge, nibble on some Asian bites and down a cocktail or two as you sink into one of the inviting sofas on the terrace overlooking Abu Dhabi's gorgeous skyline from a quieter spot at the foot of the island. The decor is retro-modern, with glowing bars, dim lighting and angular furniture throughout, and both the terrace and huge-windowed bar attract a refreshingly broad mix of clientele.

The striking view alone is worth a visit, but the extensive menu of beer, wine and cocktails, along with delicious sushi and Japanese snacks, makes this a perfect spot for both visitors and locals.

Relax@12 is also a venue that works hard to provide value to guests, with offers on throughout the week or year, weekly ladies' nights, and regular Club So-Hi nights.

Also in Aloft, check out the ridiculously popular Liquid Rain Pool Parties at Mai Cafe. Held on a regular basis, weather permitting, they were twice voted Abu Dhabi's Best Club Night.

GOT 'M' YET?

We could all do with a little "Mmmm" in our lives. Introducing the 'M' card, Marina Mall Abu Dhabi new loyalty card that allows our customers to earn points and redeem them instantly. To learn more about the benefits and to sign-up, please visit the Registration Desks at Marina Mall or **www.marinamall.ae**.

f /MarinaMallAbuDh

🐦 @MarinaMallAD

📷 @MarinaMallAD

Shopping
Spots

Shopping

Shopping

The Galleria

Shopping
Spots
Introduction

With souks, boutiques and mammoth malls at every turn, you won't have any problems spending your hard-earned cash while out and about in Abu Dhabi.

Abu Dhabi provides many opportunities to indulge in a shopping spree; with countless malls, souks and markets to choose from, the desert city is a true shopaholic's dream where you can buy just about anything and everything.

Mega-malls such as Yas Mall and Marina Mall are famed as gleaming hubs of trade filled with a mix of international high street brands and plush designer names. Practicality plays a large part in the local mall culture and, during the hotter months, these malls are oases of cool in the sweltering city – somewhere to walk, shop, eat and be entertained away from the soaring heat outside.

But shopping in Abu Dhabi is not purely about mall-trawling. Indeed, some of the city's best shopping spots are to be found outside the malls – venture a bit further and you can find yourself in an atmospheric souk shopping for gold. The souks, Arabia's traditional market places, provide a slightly more original way to shop; bargaining is very much a part of the experience and, instead of branded shops, you'll find small independent shopkeepers and stalls marketing their wares in an atmospheric setting.

In addition to specialist souks, there are a number of places where a broad range of items, including souvenirs and traditional gifts, are sold. Shopping spots around Electra Street and Hamdan Bin Mohammed Street are examples of places where you can shop to your heart's content in a non-mall setting.

Bargaining is still common practice in the souks and other traditional shopping areas of the UAE; you'll need to give it a go to get the best prices. Before you take the plunge, try to get an idea of prices from a few shops, as there can often be a significant difference. Once you've decided how much you are willing to spend, offer an initial bid that is roughly around half that price. Stay laidback and vaguely disinterested in general. When your initial offer is rejected (and it will be), keep going until you reach an agreement or until you have reached your own limit. If the price isn't right, say so and walk out – the vendor will often follow and suggest a compromise price. As a general rule, the more you buy, the better the discount. When the price is agreed, it is considered bad form to back out of the sale.

Shopping Hours
The UAE is the world capital of shopping and, with most shops open seven days a week, you'll have no trouble tracking down the goods you desire. With most malls open from around 9am until at least 10pm every night, and some until midnight at the weekends, there's plenty of time to browse.

O1 Yas Mall

Location Yas Leisure Drive, Yas Island **Web** yasmall.ae
Tel 800 927 6255 **Times** 10am-10pm (Saturday to Wednesday),
10am-midnight (weekends)
Map 1 p.222

The Abu Dhabi mall scene doesn't get any bigger, newer, or flashier than this. With 2.5 million sq ft of retail and entertainment space, Yas Mall is the second-biggest mall in the country, while its Zara, Nike, H&M and Adidas stores are the largest in the Middle East. If it's shopping you're after, you'll have your pick of over 400 stores. Movies? There's a 20-screen cinema complex. Groceries? Yas Mall has the city's largest hypermarket, French chain Geant. And if you want to keep the kids busy, there's FunWorks, a great indoor play zone focused on educational entertainment and fun.

The extensive restaurant and cafe list includes Abu Dhabi's first Cheesecake Factory, as well as additional branches of ever-popular Shake Shack, Shakespeare and Co, and Paul Cafe. If you've got a craving for sweets, Alison Nelson Chocolate Bar and the Godiva Cafe give the sugar boost needed to navigate the remainder of the mall.

With a location just off Yas Leisure Drive and 10,000 parking spaces, Yas Mall is easier to reach than some of the capital's smaller shopping areas. Just make sure you remember where you parked the car.

The popular Yas Island neighbourhood is certainly coming together, with Yas Mall directly connected to Ferrari World and a stone's throw away from the Yas Marina Circuit, Yas Waterworld, and the dining complex surrounding the attractive Yas Marina.

Al Bawadi & Al Qaws Souks

Location Bawadi Mall, Al Ain
Web bawadimall.com **Map** 2 p.211

If you make the journey to Abu Dhabi's second city, Al Ain, this souk and market is a must-see attraction. The modern complex was purpose-built to accommodate the move of the old livestock market from the town centre a few years ago. While the livestock is no longer sold from the back of broken-down pick-ups balancing on stilts, the charm of the old souk has been maintained in this new environment. As is often the case, it's the characters of the people that create the atmosphere – and that remains the same.

The animal pens are neatly lined up under shaded protection and generally sectioned by type and breed. There's a great variety of typical Emirati farming animals on display, from new-born goats and camels to enormous dairy cows and shorn sheep. You won't get crowds of tourists here – this really is an authentic local trading experience and a wonderful insight into the rural business of purchasing and trading livestock and agricultural goods.

As well as the livestock, the souk area offers over 50 stalls of traditional and agricultural items such as fertilisers, firewood, nursery plants, pet supplies and fencing, as well as vet services and small cafes.

Revisit the past at Bawadi Mall's Heritage Village – an indoor-outdoor souk selling merchandise such as gold, handicrafts, carpets, pottery and more. Or, stay in the present and visit the mall's entertainment centre with its cinema and bowling alley.

O3
The Gold Souk

Location Madinat Zayed Shopping Centre & Gold Souk
Web madinatzayed-mall.com
Times 10am-11pm (Saturday-Thursday); 4pm-11pm (Friday)
Map 3 p.213

Unfortunately, the more traditional old gold souk burnt down several years ago; to get your hands on glittering goodies now, you'll need to head for the Madinat Zayed Shopping Centre, which is where you'll find the gold centre, or gold souk.

Even without precious metals, the main centre is worth a visit. It has more than 400 outlets selling just about everything, from home accessories to clothing. The quality is varied, and some of the goods you'll discover are hilarious. But the gold centre, adjacent to the main mall, glitters with the finest gold, diamond and pearl jewellery spread across more than 100 shops. Retailers here base their prices on the daily gold market, so there's no room for bartering, but they also charge for workmanship, and here's where you can do some haggling. Most experts in the art of bargaining reckon that you can get better value for money here than in Dubai's famous gold souk, making it a great place to pick up the traditional souvenir of a pendant with your name engraved in Arabic.

The supervised toddlers' area and the games arcade will also keep the kids entertained. Meanwhile, the popular LuLu hypermarket sells everything from clothing, jewellery to home wares and groceries and is conveniently open from 8am to midnight. In truth, this is an interesting one-stop shopping destination.

04

Dalma Mall

Location Industrial City of Abu Dhabi 1 **Web** dalmamall.ae
Tel 02 550 6111 **Times** 10am-10pm (Sunday to Wednesday),
10am-midnight (Thursday to Saturday)
Map 4 p.218

Located off the island in Mussafah, Dalma Mall is a fairly new shopping complex that was built to cater to the residents of Mohammed Bin Zayed City. It has become a favourite destination for anyone living or staying off the island and wanting to avoid battling the downtown traffic.

The mall is anchored by Carrefour, Home Centre, Matalan and one of the country's biggest Marks & Spencer stores – all of which are reasons to visit in their own right. Lovers of the latest fashions will find Dalma Mall to be one of the best places to pick up threads, with all the top international high street brands, like H&M, American Eagle and Topshop, under one roof.

There are also huge offerings from Debenhams and Jumbo Electronics, as well as the only Abu Dhabi location of Pottery Barn, a popular purveyor of shabby-chic housewares.

As for entertainment, there is an international food court that has branches of Soy Express, Koala, Special Juice Bar and Yogen Früz, with seating for 500 visitors. Mall-goers can enjoy blockbusters at the giant 14-screen CineStar Cineplex, while kids will love the FunCity playzone.

05

Mushrif Mall

Location Al Mushrif, Shk Rashid bin Saeed St **Web** mushrifmall.com
Tel 02 690 4422 **Times** 10am-10pm (Sunday to Wednesday);
10am-11pm (Thursday to Saturday) **Map 5** p.215

Mushrif Mall is relatively new, and its location in the centre of the island near Mushrif Park, combined with accessible parking has made it popular with locals and expats alike.

Home to more than 200 shops, the mall is anchored by the ever-popular LuLu hypermarket. Matalan, Splash, Tchibo and Daiso all offer a variety of clothing and home accessories for budget-conscious shoppers, while US imports Naturalizer, The Body Shop and Clarks are some of the well-known higher-end brands. Shoppers looking for top brands at bottom prices would be wise to check out the capital's only outlet of The Deal.

If you get peckish while shopping, the eateries here go a little further than the bog standard food court offerings, with India Palace, Lemongrass Thai Restaurant, Jimmy's Killer Prawns, and T.G.I Friday offering substantial and higher quality fare.

Mushrif Mall is particularly popular thanks to its produce, fish and meat markets. Accessible through the basement car park, the markets offer fresh, top-quality items in a clean, air-conditioned environment that makes for an easier, though less authentic, shopping experience than the traditional souks at Meena Zayed Port.

WTC Mall and Souk

Location World Trade Center Abu Dhabi **Web** wtcad.ae
Tel 800 25327 **Times** 10am-10pm (Saturday to Wednesday); 10am-11pm
(Thursday and Friday) **Map** **6** p.213

Built on the site of the city's old souk, the opening of the World Trade Center Souk and the adjacent World Trade Center Mall have revitalised the city centre with their eclectic mix of shops, restaurants, and rooftop cafes.

The architecture of the souk is stunning, combining elements of traditional Arabia with something altogether more modern to create a maze of wooden hallways and partitions set over three storeys – a modern reinterpretation of the traditional souk. The mall takes the same theme and modernises it even further to create a bright shiny mall with a few throwback touches. Don't miss the lovely roof terrace connecting both buildings; the scene is especially beautiful at night.

The shops in the souk are one of the best places to find souvenir gifts and regional artefacts, and the rooftop cafes are popular spots for shisha. Next door to the mall, you'll find a plethora of high-end stores – it's anchored by the first Middle East outpost of House of Fraser – as well as a Spinneys market, a bookstore, a medical clinic and a superb children's play area.

10 Other Malls Not to Miss

Abu Dhabi Mall Map **11** p.214
abudhabi-mall.com
Al Ain Mall Map **12** p.211
alainmall.net
Al Wahda Mall Map **13** p.214
alwahda-mall.com
Boutik Sun & Sky Towers Map **14** p.215
sorouh.com
Deerfields Town Square Map **15** p.223
deerfieldstownsquare.com
Fotouh Al Khair Map **16** p.213
fotouhalkhair.com
Khalifa Centre Map **17** p.214
Al Zahiyah
Khalidiyah Mall Map **18** p.213
khalidiyahmall.com
Multibrand Map **19** p.214
alshaya.com
Souk Al Zafarana Map **20** p.211
Al Ain

Sougha is a government-supported initiative to encourage the preservation of traditional Emirati craftsmanship, and as such all items are handmade by female Emirati artisans. A stand on the first floor of the World Trade Center Souk sells lovely bracelets, bags and candles.

Fish, Fruit and Vegetable Souks

Location Al Meena **Times** 4.30am onwards
Map 7 p.224

Fish doesn't get much fresher than
this. The day's catch is loaded onto
the quayside and sold wholesale for
the first two hours of trading (usually
4.30 to 6.30). Then the market vendors
move on to smaller quantities after
6.30. If you want to be munching on
the best fish by lunchtime (there are
several restaurants where the chef
will happily fry up your seafood), then
you'll need to be at the market early.

While the atmosphere is electric, it
is not a place for the faint-hearted, as
the smell can be pretty strong. Across
the road from the Fish Souk is the Al
Meena Fruit and Vegetable Souk – a
much more relaxed affair. The price
and quality of the stock is often better
than in the supermarkets but, once
again, arrive early to buy the best fish
caught that morning.

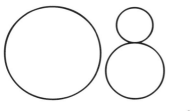

Iranian Souk

Location Al Meena **Times** 10am onwards
Map 8 p.224

It isn't air-conditioned, you won't find any convenient entertainment for the kids, and the facilities are basic to say the least, but if it's a taste of authentic Arabian trading you're after, then the Iranian Souk is the place to go.

Every few days, fresh batches of goods arrive on the dhows or barges from Iran and find their way to these shops. Everything is on sale, from household goods and traditional terracotta urns to decorative metal, cane and glass items.

The quality of the goods very much depends on how long it has been since the last load came off the boats – get lucky, and you could find some fantastic regional keepsakes or decorative items; if it's been a while, then pickings will be slim indeed.

If you're anxious for a bit of green in the desert, head to the adjacent Plant Souk. A brief stroll through the cramped aisles of trees, shrubs and flowering plants will convince you that you're in a South Asian jungle rather than a patch of concrete next to the port. Prices here are also a good deal cheaper than anywhere else.

> Haggle some more at the Carpet Souk on Al Meena Road, home to Yemeni mattresses and carpets.

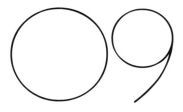

The Galleria

Location Abu Dhabi Global Market Square, Al Maryah Island
Web thegalleria.ae **Tel** 02 616 6999 **Times** 10am-10pm
(Saturday to Wednesday); 12pm-12am (Friday) **Map** 9 p.214

Fashion Avenue is to the Dubai Mall what The Galleria is to Abu Dhabi: a trendy, upscale area with only the most elite of shops. The difference: Fashion Avenue is only a section of that mall, while luxury shopping comprises the entirety of this delightfully high-end mall.

Built on the coastline of one of the newly developed islands, The Galleria's outdoor boardwalk offers a a spectacular view of the Abu Dhabi skyline. Inside, the mall's relatively simple layout holds seemingly all of the world's top brands, from Balenciaga and Burberry to Michael Kors and Mulberry. If it has been in the pages of Vogue, chances are it has a store at The Galleria. Serious shoppers from all over the globe come for the personalized concierge shopping experience that the mall offers; for the rest of us, window shopping is always available.

Fittingly, the mall's restaurants are also top-notch, from Moroccan Al Maz by Momo to Japanese standout Zuma. And Magnolia Bakery's famous banana pudding is sure to raise the sugar levels of weary shoppers.

10

Marina Mall

Location Breakwater **Web** marinamall.ae
Tel 02 681 2310 **Times** 10am-10pm (Saturday to Wednesday),
10am-12pm (Thursday and Friday) **Map** 10 p.212

Situated out on the Breakwater, but still within easy reach of the Corniche and the city's main hotels, this mall offers a breath of fresh (sea) air to its customers, especially those looking for a mix of familiar western brands with a few individual boutiques and a sprinkling of local goods, particularly on the upper level where you'll find shops specialising in traditional Arabian dress.

Other popular outlets include global favourites, such as Carrefour, Plug-Ins, Sun & Sand Sports and Woolworths. Restaurants, fast food outlets and coffee shops aplenty offer fuel for weary shoppers, while committed bargain hunters should pencil in a couple of visits during the big sale period that lasts from mid-January to the end of February.

If you get bored of shopping, the nine-screen Cinestar complex, Fun City, and the musical fountains near the main entrance will keep you entertained. There's also one of the city's biggest bowling centres and a small ice rink, while those with a taste for heights and views can have a coffee or a bite to eat in the mall's viewing tower.

On the same plot but with a separate entrance is the large Centrepoint department store, where you'll find everything from fashion and baby items to a home and garden shop. Plus, a welcome addition to the mall was CityStore, which was the region's first stand-alone shop for an English Premium League team. The Manchester City FC shop features a full range of club merchandise.

Dusit Thani
ABU DHABI

Graciously Tha
in the Heart o
Abu Dhab

For more information, please call +971 2 698 8888
or email reservations.abudhabi@dusit.com

www.Dusit.com

Destination
Hotels

Hotels

Shangri-La Qaryat Al Beri

Destination
Hotels
Introduction

If there is a single element that has come to define Abu Dhabi city and emirate, it has to be its range of breathtakingly beautiful hotels.

The hotels of Abu Dhabi don't only provide accommodation options and conference facilities, but are in fact the hubs around which the local social scenes revolve. Hotels in Abu Dhabi are places to grab a quick drink and dine in the best restaurants. They are also idyllic settings to relax in a spa, lie on the beach or take part in a huge variety of activities and watersports.

Today, almost all of the world's leading hotel brands can be found in Abu Dhabi and, given just how significant a role hotels play in the lives of those living in or visiting the region, many of those brands choose the city for showcasing their top hotels, housed in some of the region's most iconic buildings.

Abu Dhabi has been built on luxurious indulgence as much as the profits of oil and the hotels have come to symbolise that fact. You'll find some of the world's biggest hotels, its most expensive hotels, hotels that straddle golf courses, F1 circuits, mangroves, deserts and kilometres of golden beaches, as well as hotels that sit on islands which, until just a few years ago, were deserted. The hotels of Abu Dhabi have welcomed kings, queens, rock stars, heads of government and A-listers from Hollywood.

Whether you are fortunate enough to stay in one of these amazing hotels or have decided to stay elsewhere, you're sure to spend many hours in and around Abu Dhabi's top destination hotels. They are where you'll find some of the emirate's top

attractions, bars and restaurants, from the perfect race weekend views of the Yas Viceroy, luxurious Thai pampering at the Dusit Thani to the waterside venue of Shangri-La at Qaryat Al Beri.

The famous Friday brunch is a big deal in almost all of these hotels and is a great way to see a hotel or two if you're not staying there. Meanwhile, a number of these hotels sit right on their own private beaches; visitors can usually pay for a day pass that entitles you to spend the day on the beach, relax in the sunloungers, take a splash in the pool and enjoy other facilities. Nestled discreetly in the dramatic Empty Quarter – the world's largest stretch of uninterrupted sand – hotels in the nearby desert are also high on any visitor's must-stay list. Many offer a luxurious take on the Bedouin experience, including henna painting, and camel riding, along with traditionally-themed brunches and dinners. They all tend to have family-friendly facilities too, such as kids' clubs. So, make sure you see as many of Abu Dhabi's stunning destination hotels as you possibly can during your stay here. They are some of the city's greatest and most memorable attractions.

One Site Fits All
The Abu Dhabi Tourism Authority portal, visitabudhabi.com, is a one-stop-shop for hotels, featuring all of the city's main properties and the latest room rates. You can also book rooms through the site.

Yas Viceroy

Location Yas Island West
Web viceroyhotelsandresorts.com
Tel 02 656 0000
Map 1 p.222

Befitting an establishment that first opened its doors for the debut Abu Dhabi F1 Grand Prix in 2009, the Yas Viceroy spans the race track. The two halves of the hotel sit on either side of the track and are connected by a bridge over the circuit. It is both an architectural classic and an Abu Dhabi icon, especially when the distinctive shell is illuminated at dusk.

The luxurious Viceroy Group has created a hotel that is utterly modern but equally lavish and welcoming. Rooms and suites are vast and all enjoy incredible views over the race track and surrounding Yas Island.

The seven restaurants – spanning high-end seafood to luxury Middle Eastern cuisine and sushi – are all individually worth a visit at any time, but especially during race weekends, when diners can watch drivers tackle some of the circuit's most demanding corners. For something truly unique, head to Rush cocktail bar, spectacularly housed in the bridge.

The two rooftop pools and pool bars are otherworldly locations, and the roof is home to the amazing Skylite lounge and club. There's also a spa where you can enjoy pampering treatments from the UK's renowned ESPA range.

02
Emirates Palace

Location Al Ras Al Akhdar **Web** kempinski.com
Tel 02 690 9000 **Map** 2 p.212

Arguably one of Abu Dhabi's most famous landmark, the $5bn Emirates Palace boasts 392 opulent rooms and suites, all decked out with the latest technology and in a sumptuous decor.

Built and designed in colour schemes that reflect the different shades of the desert, gold and marble are scattered throughout. In total, there are more than 1,000 chandeliers. If you are feeling lavish, stay in the Palace Grand Suite, which covers 700 sq m and is a bargain at just over Dhs.40,000 per night!

The hotel sits in almost 100 hectares of gardens, which include a private marina, tennis courts, two huge swimming pools, a 1.5km private stretch of sandy beach, and sports pitches. Their opulent Emirates Spa, has one of the country's biggest Turkish hammams, while the hotel has some of the best restaurants, bars and nightspots in the capital.

If you're not lucky enough to stay at Emirates Palace but would still like to soak up its charms, the afternoon high tea is a must.

03

Anantara Sir Bani Yas Resorts

Location Al Gharbia,
Sir Bani Yas Island
Web anantara.com
Tel 02 801 5400 **Map 3** p.210

Half nature reserve, half luxury resort, Sir Bani Yas Island was developed as a nature reserve by the late Sheikh Zayed. Today, the island is an Arabian wildlife park and home to over 10,000 roaming animals and a trio of distinct Anantara properties: the Desert Islands Resort and Spa, Al Yamm Villa Resort, and their newest, Al Sahel Villas.

Probably one of the most unique resorts anywhere in the world, the island is accessible only by boat or by Rotana Jet, which leaves from Al Bateen Airport. Once you arrive at your Island hideaway, luxurious leisure awaits – from stylish rooms and private beach villas at Al Yamm to an African adventure at Al Sahel Villas, the only one of the three properties to be located inside the wildlife park. Whichever resort you choose, it's guaranteed to feel a world away from Abu Dhabi.

Anantara offers a fabulous range of excursions that take advantage of the island's unique features and mesmerising attributes. Spot animals on a nature walk or with a 4WD safari, explore a 6th century monastery, or try your hand at archery.

An island of blissful experiences awaits your arrival

Anantara Sir Bani Yas Island
Al Sahel Villa Resort

Desert Islands Resort & Spa
by Anantara

Anantara Sir Bani Yas Island
Al Yamm Villa Resort

Just off the coast of Abu Dhabi, Sir Bani Yas Island is a unique island retreat, long known for its natural and rugged beauty. Be inspired by a range of outdoor activities at Desert Islands Resort & Spa by Anantara. Immerse yourself in Arabian traditions as you enjoy views of the beachfront and lagoons at Anantara Sir Bani Yas Island Al Yamm Villa Resort, or catch sight of bountiful free-roaming animals while trekking to or from the doorstep of the extraordinary Anantara Sir Bani Yas Island Al Sahel Villa Resort.

Rates start from AED 1,050* per night including breakfast

Embark on a journey rich with discovery at **anantara.com**
Call +971 (0)2 656 1399 or crome@anantara.com

*Rates are subject to 10% service charge and 6% tourism fee. Conditions apply. Rate quoted is for stays at Desert Islands Resort & Spa by Anantara.

United Arab Emirates · Cambodia · China · Indonesia · Maldives · Mozambique · Thailand · Vietnam

global hotel alliance

Anantara
HOTELS · RESORTS · SPAS

04
Eastern Mangroves

Location Eastern Ring Road
Web anantara.com **Tel** 02 656 1000
Map 4 p.215

Located on the east coast of Abu Dhabi island, just 20 minutes from the Corniche in one direction and the airport in the other, Eastern Mangroves Hotel and Spa is Anantara's first city-based hotel in the Middle East. From the traditional Emirati welcome to the elegant fixtures and fittings, this is an oasis of tranquility in the heart of the city.

Simply look out past the lovely pool to see why it is also a one-of-a-kind destination hotel: the property lies right next to the beautiful mangroves that flank Abu Dhabi island. While the business district may only be a few minutes' drive away, the view here is of nothing but endless water, trees and shrubs – with not a single skyscraper in sight. Many of the rooms, which are luxurious, large and unfussy, share this view.

When you're not relaxing in the resort, there are plenty of leisure activities and facilities on offer, many of which take advantage of the hotel's enviable location within the lush natural environment. There is an on-site marina from which guests can access the local canals for a spot of sailing, kayaking and bird-watching. Alternatively, those in search of active pursuits can also enjoy organised excursions to some of the city's most popular attractions, from horse-riding at the Abu Dhabi Equestrian Club to the green at the Abu Dhabi Golf Club.

After such adventures, dine at the exquisite BOA Steakhouse. With a menu created just for meat connoisseurs (imagine limited edition Miyazaki Wagyu cuts), this a very special venue indeed. Or, unwind with a relaxing treat in the stunning Anantara spa, renowned around the world for its luxurious signature treatments, including a modern twist on the traditional Turkish hammam.

There is a walkway directly in front of the hotel that leads along the mangroves and right into the city. Better still, you can rent a kayak and explore the mangroves and the marine wildlife from on top of the water.

O5

Qasr Al Sarab

Location Liwa Oasis
Web anantara.com
Tel 02 656 1399 **Map** 5 p.210

One of the most sensational wilderness resorts in the world, Qasr Al Sarab Desert Resort by Anantara is an epic citadel deep in the sand-sea hinterland of the Rub Al Khali, or Empty Quarter, the world's largest sand desert. So incredible is the sight of this Arabian fort rising from the ocean of dunes, you would be forgiven for thinking that you'd stumbled onto a Hollywood set.

Walled, turreted, scattered with palm trees and featuring giant wooden doors, the main body of the resort sits within one huge complex.

A visit to Qasr Al Sarab is all about complete escape, despite being only 90 minutes from the city. There is a gorgeous pool area with a swim-up bar and a variety of day beds just begging to be sprawled across as guests take in the wonder of the surrounding dunes. Inside, the luxurious rooms are huge, with oversized bathtubs that merit at least half an hour or so of your downtime. The delicious Middle Eastern and BBQ restaurants are also deserving of some attention, and the seasonal Bedouin-style dinners are not to be missed.

Anantara Spa celebrates Arabian traditions as hammam baths lie amid peaceful courtyards beneath natural red dunes. The hotel also arranges dune bashing adventures and romantic dinners under the stars.

Create a thousand timeless moments in a luxury **desert** oasis

قصر السراب
QASR AL SARAB
منتجع و مناظر الواحة الصحراء
Desert Resort by Anantara

Unwind in palatial comfort surrounded by the towering sand dunes of Abu Dhabi's legendary Liwa desert in Qasr Al Sarab Desert Resort by Anantara. Follow in the footsteps of the ancient Bedouin on exciting desert escapades, rejuvenate body and mind with indulgent spa experiences and dine on mouth-watering cuisine as you admire the breathtaking views. Escape to a luxurious desert retreat that blends epic Arabian adventure with tranquil splendour, and create memories that will last a lifetime.

Rates start from AED 1,200* per night including breakfast.

Embark on a journey rich with discovery at **anantara.com**
Call +971 (0)2 656 1399 or crome@anantara.com for enquiries and reservations.

*Rates are subject to 10% service charge and 6% tourism fee. Subject to availability.

United Arab Emirates · Cambodia · China · Indonesia · Maldives · Mozambique · Thailand · Vietnam

Anantara
HOTELS · RESORTS · SPAS

global hotel alliance

St Regis Saadiyat Island Resort

Location Saadiyat Island **Web** stregissaadiyatisland.com
Tel 02 498 8888 **Map** 6 p.225

If you're looking to escape the bustle of Abu Dhabi without leaving the city, the St Regis Saadiyat Island Resort is a top choice. Located on the pristine Saadiyat beachfront, the well-appointed rooms have views of either the turquoise gulf waters or the greens of the Saadiyat Beach Golf Club. Balconies on each room allow guests to take in fresh air alongside the amazing vistas.

The beach itself is the biggest draw for this hotel. One of the capital's only natural beaches, it is truly postcard-perfect. The hotel provides chairs, umbrellas, and menu service, making for a hassle-free experience. If you tire of the sand, there are also three outdoor pools, an indoor lap pool, an above-average spa and gym, and a kids' club, meaning that you'll be hard pressed to feel bored.

Despite its somewhat remote location, the hotel has easy access to top restaurants, shops, salons, and a grocery store via its on-site retail complex The Collection. Convenient, because with an environment this peaceful, you won't want to leave.

A true beach resort that's quite unlike any other hotel in Abu Dhabi, the St Regis looks more like a Californian retreat. Perfect as an escape from the city. Stop here and dine at the popular 5th The Grill.

07

Fairmont Bab Al Bahr

Location Al Maqta **Web** fairmont.com/BabAlBahr
Tel 02 654 3333 **Map** 7 p.217

Views of the Sheikh Zayed Grand Mosque, handcrafted delights at the Chocolate Gallery or dining at the phenomenally good Marco Pierre White's Steakhouse and Grill, there are reasons aplenty to stay at the well-located Fairmont Bab Al Bahr.

Luxurious rooms aside, there's also a collection of stunning outdoor pools overlooking the spectacular creek, as well as a covered children's pool and Jacuzzi. The pool bar is the perfect setting for sundowners, especially during happy hour. The hotel's bars and restaurants are a massive draw, from Italian at Frankie's for romantic dining, to casual alfresco Lebanese at Cedar Lounge. The all-day CuiScene has international appeal.

For the ultimate break, book a Fairmont Gold room to enjoy additional privileges such as Gold Lounge access for breakfast and afternoon tea, a butler on call, and evening drinks and hors d'oeuvres.

Dusit Thani

Location Al Wahdah **Web** dusit.com
Tel 02 698 8888 **Map** 8 p.214

The Thai chain's latest UAE offering has an incredibly impressive atrium – it is one of the tallest in the world. Well-equipped for business travellers, it has a huge conference centre, 402 rooms and suites and 131 furnished executive apartments. For passing tourists too, there's a great rooftop pool and well-equipped gym if you are keen to keep fit before you indulge and indulge you might because there are some fantastic dining options here. For traditional Thai, book a table at their signature restaurant, Benjarong, or for a meat feast, the Capital Grill scores highly. Be sure to factor in a visit to the excellent Namm Spa to sample an extensive range of indulgent Thai massages and revitalising body scrubs.

On the exterior, the Dusit Thani Abu Dhabi's prominent glass tower punctuates the skyline perfectly at a convenient location in the capital's business and government district. Its innovative architectural design blends well on the urban landscape yet it is only a stone's throw from away from the city's lush natural mangroves, the Corniche and Abu Dhabi's stunning and iconic sea front promenade.

09
Shangri-La Qaryat Al Beri

Location Al Maqta **Web** shangri-la.com
Tel 02 509 8888
Map 9 p.217

The Arabian-inspired architecture and decor of the Shangri-La Qaryat Al Beri are enough to make it a destination hotel of the highest order; however, as well as the superb, luxurious facilities and first-class service, it is the location that makes this hotel really stand out from the pack.

The resort looks out over the narrow creek that separates Abu Dhabi island from the mainland. The 214 spacious rooms and suites capitalise on this unique setting; all boast private terraces that have stunning views over the creek and to the island, where the Sheikh Zayed Grand Mosque stands majestically. Elsewhere in the hotel, there are two gyms, five swimming pools, and a one-kilometre stretch of private, golden beach.

The beautiful spa and welcoming outlets – particularly Bord Eau and P&C by Sergi Arola – are extremely popular with the city's most fashionable guests and residents looking for an atmospheric night by the water's edge. As if this weren't enough, the Shangri-La has direct access into the Souk at Qaryat Al Beri, an Arabian-style souk.

10

Westin Abu Dhabi Golf Resort & Spa

Location Sas Al Nakhl **Web** westinabudhabigolfresort.com
Tel 02 616 9999 **Map** 10 p.218

Abu Dhabi has become a top destination for golfing enthusiasts, and the Westin Abu Dhabi Golf Resort & Spa is a favourite among visitors looking to pursue their hobby. If you dream of improving your short game or spending half the day practising your drives, this hotel will suit you down to a tee.

The resort is located in the middle of the world-renowned Abu Dhabi Golf Club, with its 27-hole championship course, where some of the biggest names compete in the Abu Dhabi HSBC Golf Championship each year. The Heavenly Spa, a lagoon-like main pool and children's facilities will help you relax afterwards.

The hotel's food and drink outlets have an excellent reputation, with the Moroccan-inspired restaurant, Agadir, and the cocktail and wine bar Lemon & Lime both attracting visitors from all over the emirates. The Bubbalicious Brunch, held every Friday with a wide range of live cooking stations and free flowing Louis Roederer, is fast becoming one of the top brunches in the capital.

Spas

Hammam at Eastern Mangroves

Spas
Introduction

Abu Dhabi and luxurious pampering go together like strawberries and cream, or the desert and camels, and you'll find spas of all sizes and styles ready to rub, scrub and knead you into relaxation.

Whether you've just arrived and are in need of a long, lazy day of pampering to help ease you into your vacation, or you have a specific knot that needs to be worked out, someone, somewhere in Abu Dhabi will have the necessary facilities and skills to have you feeling better in no time. Pampering is big business here, from the cavernous spas of the biggest hotels to the beautifying villas of the Bateen area, plus all the smaller, boutique massage centres dotted throughout the city.

There are also numerous massage and relaxation techniques available, with prices and standards varying. The opulent five-star hotels will obviously customise every detail for a blissful experience – and a massage at these usually means you can wallow in Jacuzzis, saunas and steam rooms before and after your treatment – but you'll pay top dollar. There are plenty of independent places that offer better value for money, but you will have to forego some of the more luxurious facilities. Plenty of hotels have spas pitched somewhere in the middle too.

For a typical Arabian pampering experience, opt for an Oriental hammam. This treatment is traditional in the Middle East region and shares similarities with Turkish baths. The name refers to the bath (the room) in which the treatment takes place – typically an elaborate affair on Abu Dhabi's five-star spa scene. A hammam involves a variety of different experiences, including being bathed, scrubbed and massaged on a hot table. It's an absolute must-do and the hammams at the Emirates Palace Spa or at any of the Anantara spas at Eastern Mangroves, Qasr Al Sarab and the Desert Islands Sir Bani Yas Island Resort are highly recommended. Thai treatments at the Dusit Thani's Namm Spa, facials at Sisters Beauty Lounge or at Thalgo Spa are all indulgent treats. A number of spas have couples' treatment rooms where you and your significant other can enjoy a massage at the same time. If you're the demanding type, you could even opt for a four hands massage.

For a truly unique Abu Dhabi memory, try something a little different. A number of spas offer unique signature treatments with unusual ingredients. The Westin Heavenly Spa has a caviar treatment while, not wishing to be left behind, Mosaic (mosaicspa.ae) offers a crushed olive seed scrub. Treatments at CHI at the Shangri-La sound more like a dinner menu, with Arabian date rituals, rose and honey wraps, and Arabic coffee scrubs all available.

Relaxing Prices
Some spas will offer special treatments at certain times of year, as well as reductions on treatments or packages. If you're thinking about indulging yourself, it could also be worth checking out sites like Groupon.com, which often have discounts on spa treatments.

Emirates Palace Spa

Location Emirates Palace **Web** emiratespalace.ae
Tel 02 690 9000 **Times** 10am-10pm
Map 1 p.212

As you would expect of any spa located deep inside the opulent confines of one of the world's grandest and most expensive hotels, the Emirates Palace Spa is the absolute epitome of luxury.

Pairing world-leading brands with pampering principles, an exquisite menu for men and women, combines precious elements such as gold, diamonds and minerals with ancient spa traditions, such as the royal hammam ritual, revealing a heavy Moroccan influence. The decadent spa oozes tranquility, from the aromatherapy reception trickling with water features to its private treatment rooms, elegantly kitted out with personal steam room and shower – everything you need for some indulgent me-time.

Highlights include youth promoting and skin healing, customised facials to rejuvenate skin at the cellular level, delivered with products from scientifically-proven brands, Forlle'd and Amra, while the Pedi:Mani:Cure studio employs the techniques of French foot virtuoso Bastien Gonzalez to promote inner shine. Expect a truly palatial spa experience.

> The signature Palace massage combines masterful techniques with an abundance of 24-carat gold oil to rebalance both mind and body; arguably the most indulgent spa treatment you'll find.

CHI, The Spa

Location Shangri-La Hotel
Web shangri-la.com
Tel 02 509 8900
Times 10am-midnight
Map 2 p.217

Get the energies flowing at the Shangri-La's CHI spa, a real sanctum of Zen and relaxation. Guests are advised to arrive early to make the most of the facilities, which include a spa pool, steam room, sauna and Jacuzzi – the perfect way to begin the relaxation process before your treatment.

The only real stress is trying to choose from the extensive range of luxurious scrubs, massages, facials, signature treatments and regionally inspired relaxation rituals on offer. The black soap hammam and half-day CHI experiences are particularly recommended for sinking into a state of bliss.

Thalgo Spa

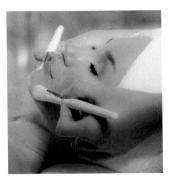

Location Abu Dhabi Country Club **Web** adcountryclub.com
Tel 02 666 8885 **Times** 10am-10pm
Map 3 p.214

The UAE is jam-packed with amazing spas but Thalgo Spa, at the popular Abu Dhabi Country Club, is by far the country's largest. The grandeur though is not its only draw, as within its sprawling 2,000 sq m there are a number of unique and hugely appealing features. For starters, Thalgo have introduced the country's first Polynesian therapies to the spa scene and their signature Mahana massage is a relaxation miracle. Thalgo's calming sea theme washes over its

23 treatment rooms, steam room and Jacuzzi, and the ocean facial is a popular option. Mellow sounds and sea-breeze smells create a restful mood and welcoming setting.

As a French brand and the high-end products are a fantastic blend of luxurious marine ingredients boosted by exquisite floral fragrances and herbal extracts. Here you'll find a dedicated nail salon and a free style treatment centre. Size is their strength and there is also an elegant VIP set-up.

04

ESPA

Location Yas Viceroy Abu Dhabi **Web** espaskincare.com
Tel 02 656 0862 **Times** 9am-9pm
Map 4 p.222

The UK brand ESPA has become
something of a byword for luxurious
indulgence and ESPA at Yas Viceroy
is almost the dictionary definition of
a modern, urban spa. From welcome
to goodbye, it's a classy operation,
but not at the cost of personalised
relaxation session.

The treatments on offer are
vast – signature treatments, facials,
dedicated male treatments, a
ladies' hammam, and more than 30
massages, wraps and scrubs – while
the range of combination journeys
and 'escapes' offer good value.
In fact, for a top-notch five-star
spa, prices at ESPA remain fairly
reasonable. However, rather than
choosing a therapy 'off the peg', you're
encouraged to provide your therapist
with information about what you
would like, and they'll tailor-make a
treatment for you.

There are nine treatment rooms,
and the separate male and female
relaxation lounges both overlook the
race track and the marina. The Viceroy
Presidential Treatment Suite features
its own hammam steam room with a
rain shower and colour therapy.

If you've a little extra
time to spare after your
spa treatment, try the
intriguing Metronap – 20
minutes spent in the
space-age recliner pod
is equal to an eight-hour
sleep, apparently.

05

Zen The Spa

Location Beach Rotana Abu Dhabi **Web** rotana.com
Tel 02 697 9000 **Times** 10am-10pm (daily)
Map 5 p.214

The Beach Rotana is one of Abu Dhabi's busiest hotels located in the bustling Al Zahiyah; however,

descending the stairs down to Zen is like disappearing into a spacious, comfy rabbit hole of relaxation. The uncluttered, minimalist approach provides a welcome respite from busy city life.

If you take your pampering seriously, there are a couple of treatment suites available; with private changing rooms, showers and colossal baths, these are luxury defined. Other facilities include lovely relaxation areas.

If it can be scrubbed, wrapped, hydrated, treated or massaged, then it's on the menu at Zen, and signature treatments, such as rejuvenation, immune-boosting, and pregnancy massages, are excellent value. Some of the specialist pampering options include a rasul mud ritual, teen treatments and massage lessons.

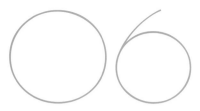

Hiltonia

Location Hilton Abu Dhabi **Web** hilton.com
Tel 02 692 4336 **Times** 10am-10pm (daily)
Map 6 p.212

A long-time favourite amongst the city's residents, the Hiltonia Health Club & Spa is a blissful haven of tranquillity set in some beautiful surroundings. The cool marble floors and ethnic decor make for a consummately soothing setting, and the spacious but well-equipped treatment rooms boast private showers to prep for your treatment or wash off the excess scrubs and oils afterwards.

As well as the aromatherapy and reflexology treatments, which are some of the best and most popular in the city, the spa also offers signature Indian head massages and an intriguing range of hydro treatments, some of which soothe the muscles while others detox the skin and target the main organs.

Alternatively, you can opt for one of the special packages, which combine body treatments with facials and nail care, and include the use of the sauna, eucalyptus steam room and Jacuzzi. The Tropical Bliss (Four Hand Massage) is 90 minutes of pure, well, bliss, and the Cleopatra Hydro Bath and Soothing Massage is an all-over treat.

07

Zayna Spa

Location Grand Millennium Al Wahda **Web** millenniumhotels.com
Tel 02 495 3822 **Times** 10am-11pm (daily)
Map 7 p.214

The exotic Asian theme is now so commonplace amongst spas that it's easy to dismiss any place that employs it as just another bog-standard massage joint. Fortunately, there are still spas like Zayna which remind us that Asia is the spiritual home of both the sumptuous spa and seven-star service.

Gentle music, a peppermint aroma and warm south-east Asian hospitality set the scene for head-to-toe pampering. Each of the 10 treatment rooms is fully-equipped with bath and changing facilities. The treatments cover the usual bases,

from luxurious facials to delightful hot stone massages. Signature packages are also available, from 30 minutes up to five hours, ideal for a quick treatment before hitting the beach or a full-blown indulgence day.

Try something new at Zayna: how about a tropical salt mousse glow to restore and re-energise the skin; an aromatherapy hydrating seaweed bath; or even a caviar facial?

Iridium Spa

Location St Regis Saadiyat Island Resort
Web stregissaadiyatisland.com **Tel** 02 498 8888 **Times** 9am-10pm
Map 8 p.227

As if spending time at one of the Saadiyat Island beach resorts wasn't relaxing enough, Iridium is the chill-out cherry on the calmness cake. The whites, beiges and browns, along with the natural stone and wood finishes used throughout both public areas and treatment rooms, give Iridium Spa an air of rustic perfection. A visit here feels like a woodland retreat as much as a therapeutic treat.

The treatment menu is fairly expansive (although, it is fair to say, Iridium is also on the pricier side) but this spa generally eschews the one-size-fits-all approach to relaxation and therapy. Based on a number of questions, each massage, scrub and wrap is tailored to the client's wants and needs. The therapists are impressively knowledgeable about the treatments, and they do a great job of making you feel utterly relaxed.

09

Mizan

Location Hilton Capital Grand Abu Dhabi
Web hilton.com
Tel 02 617 0000 **Times** 10am-10pm
Map 9 p.217

In comparison to the major hotel spas such The Ritz-Carlton and Emirates Spa, Al Maqta Hotel's Mizan spa is not particularly well known. In addition, the hotel itself is aimed predominantly at business travellers – again, something that doesn't exactly scream 'top class spa'. So Mizan comes as a real surprise, as this huge spa is one of Abu Dhabi's biggest, brightest and, arguably, best equipped.

The spa has all the usual wet zones, with saunas and Jacuzzis appearing alongside experiential showers, lovely plunge pools, a Vichy shower suite and a deluxe hammam area. The decor throughout the wet areas, ladies' and gents' separate relaxation areas and the private treatment rooms is soft, airy and spacious, creating a pleasant and relaxed mood that differs from the standard spa 'chill out'.

All the usual treatments are covered, from facials to body wraps, although the top-class therapists here perform the basic Thai and Swedish massages so well that it's hard to look past those.

10

Namm

Location Dusit Thani Abu Dhabi **Web** dusit.com/dtad
Tel 02 698 8888 **Times** 9am-9pm
Map 10 p.214

An exciting addition to the spa scene, Namm is a serene haven in a beautiful Thai setting. On arrival, its elegant decor is as soothing as your welcome sip of ginger tea. Naturally, Thai treatments top the menu and the signature Heritage Therapy uses time-tested herbal medicines, popular with Thai Royalty, to both restore and rebalance energy. This aromatherapy oil-drenched massage simultaneously relieves muscle tension and detoxifies. Or, the more invigorating Thai Harmony massage relies on deep finger pressure to alleviate muscle fatigue and is equally effective. Performed on Thai mattresses without oil, this uplifting full body massage reduces tension and improves flexibility for inner balance.

Beyond the kneading, a nourishing snow lotus and gold leaf body scrub provides anti-age benefits with liquorice extract to sooth skin, while an age-defying ice facial will boost any complexion. Using the innovative Anne Semonin neurocosmetic range, the facials here deliver *results* – a word that quite simply sums up the entire Namm Spa experience.

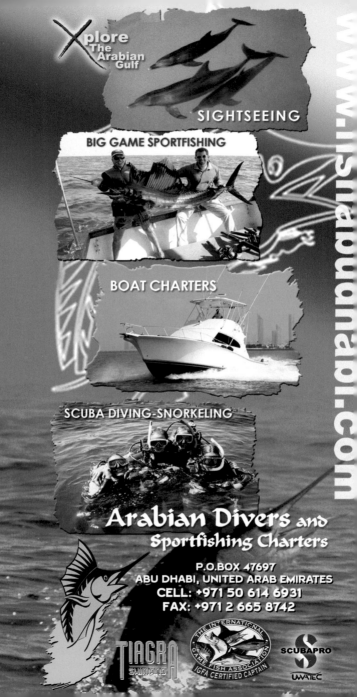

Activities

Adrenaline Activities

Desert Driving

Adrenaline
Activities
Introduction

When it comes to living the ultimate adventure, Abu Dhabi is a complete outdoor playground, with a huge number of experiences on offer.

As ever-increasing tourist numbers demonstrate, Abu Dhabi's appeal is booming with visitors from all over the world stopping in on the emirate to experience just some of what it has to offer. While glitzy malls, breath-taking hotels and gravity-defying buildings may be what many expect when they board the plane, more and more are heading for the UAE to experience some incredible activities and unique experiences. From watersports to motorsports, the choice is endless.

Where some see a vast and hypnotic desert, some people in Abu Dhabi see the world's largest adventure playground, offering sensational experiences like dune bashing, sand boarding and quad biking, as well as camping and horse or camel riding. One of the best ways to experience a variety of these is on an evening or overnight desert safari.

To really take in the majesty of the desert, those with a head for heights might like to take to the skies. An early morning hot air balloon ride is one enthralling way of doing so, while you can also jump into a small Seawings plane for a bird's eye tour of this incredible island city and beyond.

Aside from the desert and the skies, Abu Dhabi's waters also have much to excite thrill-seekers, with activities that range from scuba diving, kayaking around the mangroves to boat trips and high-octane watersports such as flyboarding. There are a number of watersports centres such as

Watercooled Abu Dhabi, Hiltonia and BAKE in Saadiyat Beach that provide the full gamut of water-based activities, but you'll also find plenty going on at the beachfront hotels.

As well as natural charms, there are plenty of man-made ones too, with the attractions out on Yas Island, arguably providing the highest thrills-per-second ratio you'll find anywhere in the Middle East. And if driving extremely fast sounds more exhilarating, try out the performance of an F1 car at the Yas Marina Circuit.

Adrenaline junkies don't need to head out to the desert or jet across to distant shores to get a taste of extreme adventure. There is a myriad of indoor attractions in the capital, which include climbing walls and simulators. Although there is no actual jumping out of planes involved, the indoor skydiving centre at Spacewalk is a thrill-seeking way to enjoy flying in the air for minutes at a time: a giant vertical wind tunnel reproduces the thrilling sensation of jumping from a plane. Plenty, then, to keep even the most ardent adrenaline junkie busy.

Desert Delights

Many of Abu Dhabi's biggest thrills can be found out in the Rub Al Khali, which is also known as the Empty Quarter. This vast desert covers 650,000 sq km of towering dunes and sprawling salt flats, making it the world's largest sand desert.

O1
Hot Air Balloon

Location Al Ain **Web** ballooning.ae
Tel 04 285 4949 **Times** Approximately 5am-6am
Price Guide Dhs.995 (per person) **Map** 1 p.211

Combining soaring skyscrapers, rolling dunes, spectacular islands and beautiful mangroves, Abu Dhabi from the air is an impressive sight. And there's nothing better than taking in the serenity of the desert from a graceful hot air balloon flight.

Balloon Adventures organises tours, with flights departing just before sunrise, although the early start is more than worthwhile once the balloon climbs to provide you with some refreshments once you do touch down, and trips are generally followed by some dune driving as you make your way back.

Of course, you never know where you're going to end up but the support team will be waiting for you with the most awe-inspiring of views.

The Yellow Boats

Location Emirates Palace Marina **Web** theyellowboats.com
Tel 800 8044 **Times** 9am-5pm (daily)
Price Guide Dhs.200 **Map** 2 p.212

If you're after an adrenaline rush on the waters of the Gulf, sign up for a turbo jet experience with The Yellow Boats. They offer exhilaratingly fast-paced tours on board eco-friendly inflatable crafts, which allow you to take in some of the best sights of the Arabian Gulf at heart-stopping speeds.

After heading out from the Breakwater and gently cruising past Lulu Island, the captain lets rip and the boat flies over the water past Abu Dhabi icons like Emirates Palace, Marina Mall, and the towers that line the Corniche, making extreme twists and turns along the way. Brace yourself, as you're bound to get a little wet, although the captain does stop at a few choice locations for you to take some holiday snaps.

As well as the Abu Dhabi tours, The Yellow Boats does a high-speed tour of Dubai Marina, if you find yourself in need of an adrenaline fix while visiting the neighbouring city.

> Slow things down and enjoy a leisurely panoramic tour of Dubai Marina by day or night with The Yellow Boats; Dhs.80 for adults and Dhs.30 for children.

03
Dune Bashing

Location Various
Times Full day or late afternoon
Price Guide Approx. Dhs.150-Dhs.350

If one activity sums up the Abu Dhabi adventure experience, it has to be dune bashing. Head out of the city in just about any direction at the weekend, and you'll find scores of locals lined up in their 4WDs about to head off on desert-driving adventures. It's so much fun that both expats and tourists have got in on the act.

For most visitors, the best way to experience a spot of dune bashing is on a desert safari. The experienced driver will amaze you with just what a 4WD vehicle is capable of doing, as it rocks, rolls, sways and surfs over the dunes in what is effectively a white-knuckle rollercoaster ride but without the rails. Overnight, full day and dune dinner trips are available.

Unfortunately, insurance doesn't cover off-road accidents so you can't just rent a 4WD and give it a go yourself. But, if you still want to get off-road, you can try your hand at quad biking or sand buggying. Many desert safaris offer quadding, while all the main tour operators can also organise a quad bike or buggy tour of the nearby desert, and Al Forsan has a dedicated off-road zone and race circuit.

04

Formula Rossa

Location Ferrari World Abu Dhabi **Web** ferrariworldabudhabi.com
Tel 02 496 8001 **Times** 11am-8pm (daily, except Mondays)
Price Guide Dhs.250 **Map** 4 p.222

Imagine a rollercoaster so fast that you have to wear safety goggles. If that sounds like your perfect adrenaline-soaked way to spend a few minutes then imagine no longer, and get yourself to Ferrari World Abu Dhabi. Here, at the world's biggest indoor theme park, you'll find Formula Rossa – the world's fastest coaster.

The sensation has to be experienced but the figures tell some of the tale: FR accelerates from 0-100kmph in two seconds, reaching the top speed of 240kmph in 4.9 seconds; riders experience an incredible 1.7Gs of G-Force at some points on the ride; this thrilling ride was modelled on the Ferrari F1 car.

Essentially, the coaster catapults you out and up to a height of 52 metres, before descending through a series of sweeping turns and chicanes that were inspired by the legendary Monza race track in Italy. At 2.2km in total length, Formula Rossa is also one of the longest coasters in the world.

High-octane rides include a 62m high ride that drops vertically through the park's roof, and a flume-style water ride that leads you through a series of twists and turns based on the workings of a Ferrari 599 engine.

Flyboarding

Locations Kite Beach, Yas Island, Five Continents Cassells
Hotel & Beach Resort and Ghantoot **Web** flyboards-uae.com
Tel 050 817 3071 **Times** Various
Price Guide From Dhs.300 for 30 minutes **Map** 5 p.222

Never heard of it? That's because flyboarding is one of the world's newest watersport crazes. Invented by a French jetski designer in 2011, it involves a boot-wearing rider who's strapped into a small board. The board is connected to a jetski via a 18m hose; when the jetski pushes water into the hose, the board and rider are elevated up to 8m.

Flyboarders with their own boards have been popping up sporadically on the Corniche, twirling and diving through the air in front of the public beach, for the past couple of years. Meanwhile, in nearby Dubai, the 2014

Flyboard World Cup took place and was a spectacle. But to really get the adrenaline pumping, of course, you'll have to try it out yourself.

Abu Dhabi Marine Sports offers private classes off Kite Beach on Yas Island. A professional instructor will give you a safety lesson and let you practise in relatively shallow, calm water before heading out deep. It's not as tricky as it looks, though balance is key. Once you master the art of staying vertical, it's time to learn flips and tricks. Make sure to have a photographer ready to capture your flight.

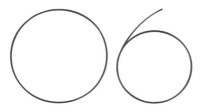

Kitesurfing

Location Various **Web** kitesurfinguae.com
Price Guide Dhs.250 (group lesson), Dhs.350 (one hour private lesson)

Kitesurfing is the most dynamic and exciting watersport on the waves and participation is booming, with kitesurfing set to become an Olympic discipline in 2016. Whether you need to learn the ropes from scratch, want a couple of refresher lessons or are already a pro and simply need to hire some equipment, Abu Dhabi is a great place to try the sport.

There are two main kiting beaches close to the city; one on Yas Island and another at Al Dabayyah, a half hour or so drive west towards Mirfa.

A few hours further west leads you to the Pearl Coast and Mirfa – another great kiting spot. Do note that none of these beaches have facilities or lifeguards, so kiting is always done at your own risk.

There are several individuals and companies in Abu Dhabi that offer kitesurfing lessons, with prices including all the equipment, such as kite, harness and board. Lessons aren't too cheap so, if you're looking to keep the cost down, taking part in small group lessons may be the way to go.

Kitepro Abu Dhabi has a school that covers basic, intermediate and advanced kitesurfing, with all the latest equipment such as radio helmets. Lessons cost Dhs.350 for 60-minutes and Kitepro know all the best shallow-water spots for beginners.

07

Spacewalk

Location Abu Dhabi Country Club
Web adcountryclub.com
Tel 02 657 7601
Times 12pm-9pm
Price Guide Dhs.180-Dhs.700
Map 7 p.214

If it's the full skydiving adventure you're after, head over to Dubai where Skydive Dubai offers thrilling tandem jumps over Palm Jumeirah (skydivedubai.ae).

The name of the Abu Dhabi Country Club perhaps conjures images of more leisurely pursuits but, in fact, this is where you'll find one of Abu Dhabi's greatest thrill rides. For anyone who isn't quite ready (or inclined) to jump out of an aeroplane, Spacewalk is the next best thing.

It is not a ride or simulator but an actual indoor skydiving experience, using a giant vertical wind tunnel to reproduce the thrilling sensation of jumping from a plane, but at a fraction of the cost.

For beginners, there's an instructor on hand to help you perfect the technique and alter the wind speed according to your size, weight and ability. However, the experience is such a fun and realistic one that even well-practised skydivers will enjoy the opportunity to perfect some moves thanks to the increased 'free fall' time. Plus, it's a great place for taking funny photos of friends and family whose faces are being distorted by the powerful column of air.

O8
Yas Marina Circuit

Location Yas Island West **Web** yasmarinacircuit.com
Tel 02 659 9800 **Times** 9am-6pm
Price Guide Formula Yas 3000 Experience from Dhs.1,500,
KartZone Experience Dhs.55-Dhs.110 **Map** 8 p.222

Ever dreamed of racing alongside Vettel or flying past Alonso on the last bend of a Formula 1 Grand Prix? The Formula Yas 3000 experience gets you pretty close. Yas Marina Circuit offers you the opportunity to strap yourself in for a thrilling race around the track.

After being given a briefing by the fully-qualified instructors, you'll be in charge of the 3000cc V6 racer. Two on-board cameras will capture the action, so that you can take home a reminder of your day.

Yas Marina Circuit has a number of other driving activities available, in cars such as a Chevrolet Camero and Aston Martin GT4. These unique passenger experiences give you the opportunity to feel the pure power and exhilaration of a three-seated drag car (which reaches 100kmph in just two seconds) with a seasoned veteran behind the wheel. The KartZone, meanwhile, offers a fleet of leisure karts that also deliver an excellent racing experience, perfect for families and groups.

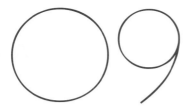

Diving

Location Marina Al Bateen Resort **Web** arabiandivers.net
Tel 050 614 6931 **Times** Various
Price Guide Various
Map 9 p.213

The warm seas and clear, calm waters of the Arabian Gulf are perfect for exploring the region's varied underwater life, and the seas around Abu Dhabi's numerous islands have a fair amount of marine creatures to discover. There are also plenty of interesting dive sites, especially wrecks, some of which are within easy reach of Abu Dhabi.

Local dive companies can get you out to these sites, as well as help you improve your diving skills, with courses offered under the usual international training organisations.

Arabian Divers & Sportfishing Charters, based in Al Bateen Marina, is one of the best known companies, with more than 20 years of experience off the coast of Abu Dhabi. As well as the boats and equipment, the company has a classroom and training pool, so even if you've never dived before arriving in Abu Dhabi, you could leave with a PADI qualification and a couple of dives in the Arabian Gulf under your diver's belt. The company also organises big game sport fishing trips throughout the year.

Prodive's new dive centre at Jebel Ali in nearby Dubai is attracting learner scuba divers with its excellent facilities. Along with beach access, catamarans, reef balls, and state of the art training equipment, Prodive boasts one of the deepest pools in Dubai for diving.

Xplore The Arabian Gulf

SIGHTSEEING

BIG GAME SPORTFISHING

BOAT CHARTERS

SCUBA DIVING-SNORKELING

Arabian Divers and Sportfishing Charters

P.O.BOX 47697
ABU DHABI, UNITED ARAB EMIRATES
CELL: +971 50 614 6931
FAX: +971 2 665 8742

www.fishabudhabi.com

TIAGRA
SHIMANO

THE INTERNATIONAL
GAME FISH ASSOCIATION
IGFA CERTIFIED CAPTAIN

SCUBAPRO
UWATEC

10
Seawings

Location Various **Web** seawings.ae
Tel 04 807 0708 **Times** Various
Price Guide From Dhs.895-Dhs.1,495

There is no denying that flying is one of the best ways to soak up the awe-inspiring skyline that Abu Dhabi and the country has become famous for. The Seawings Abu Dhabi tours fly across the capital, providing incredible views of the most iconic landmarks, including Ferrari World, Yas Marina Circuit, the Corniche, Mina Zayed Port, the mangroves and Emirates Palace. The snapshot tour leaves (and lands back) at Yas Marina or the Emirates Palace, with hotel pick ups and transfers optional. The Dubai Scenic tour, meanwhile, takes in the amazing Abu Dhabi sights before heading to Dubai and delivering aerial panoramas of Dubai Marina, Burj Khalifa, the World Islands and Palm Jumeirah. After the 40-minute trip, you are free to explore all the sights of the city back on terra firma.

Why not charter a seaplane and set out on your own dream route? Increasingly popular is the Seawings charter from Dubai's Jebel Ali Golf Resort & Spa to the idyllic Sir Bani Yas Island nature reserve or the impressive Hilton Ras Al Khaimah Resort & Spa. Whatever flight path you choose, relish the comfort of a five-star hotel and enjoy an unforgettable Seawings experience.

An island of blissful experiences awaits your *arrival*

Anantara Sir Bani Yas Island
Al Sahel Villa Resort

Desert Islands Resort & Spa
by Anantara

Anantara Sir Bani Yas Island
Al Yamm Villa Resort

Just off the coast of Abu Dhabi, Sir Bani Yas Island is a unique island retreat, long known for its natural and rugged beauty. Be inspired by a range of outdoor activities at Desert Islands Resort & Spa by Anantara. Immerse yourself in Arabian traditions as you enjoy views of the beachfront and lagoons at Anantara Sir Bani Yas Island Al Yamm Villa Resort, or catch sight of bountiful free-roaming animals while trekking to or from the doorstep of the extraordinary Anantara Sir Bani Yas Island Al Sahel Villa Resort.

Rates start from AED 1,050* per night including breakfast

Embark on a journey rich with discovery at **anantara.com**
Call +971 (0)2 656 1399 or crome@anantara.com

*Rates are subject to 10% service charge and 6% tourism fee. Conditions apply. Rate quoted is for stays at Desert Islands Resort & Spa by Anantara.

United Arab Emirates · Cambodia · China · Indonesia · Maldives · Mozambique · Thailand · Vietnam

global hotel alliance

Anantara
HOTELS · RESORTS · SPAS

Places In The Sun

Beachside Watersports

Places In The Sun
Introduction

Abu Dhabi has no shortage of places for beachgoers to head to in order to top up their tan, or for outdoor enthusiasts to enjoy the year-round sunshine.

During the cooler months, there are some excellent outdoor options to discover across Abu Dhabi. In fact, there are so many alfresco delights, you might be tempted to never step inside a mall or a hotel during the winter. The green parks are superbly maintained, while the beaches draw crowds of sunbathers and swimmers, particularly at weekends. But that's not all; there's plenty of fun to be had beyond the city limits too. And, even though you're unlikely to tire of enjoying the urban attractions, there are a couple of huge adventure playgrounds – in the form of the desert and the Arabian Gulf – just waiting to be explored.

There's no doubt that Abu Dhabi's beaches are some of the main attractions for sun-seeking visitors. Blessed with warm weather, calm ocean waters and long stretches of sand, the emirate's beaches come in various types, depending on requirement. Choose from public beaches (limited facilities but no entry fee), the Corniche beach parks (good facilities and a nominal entrance fee), or private beaches (normally part of a hotel or resort). Regulations for public beaches are quite strict, but that's not necessarily a bad thing. Dogs are banned, for instance, and so is driving, therefore the sand is kept clean. Other off-limit activities include barbecues, camping without a permit and holding large parties.

Abu Dhabi is also home to a number of excellent parks, with lush green lawns and a variety of trees creating the perfect escape from the concrete city. Mushrif Central Park has just been refurbished and has a petting zoo, jogging track and more. Most parks have a kiosk or cafe selling snacks and drinks, and some have barbecue pits. Regulations at parks vary, with some banning bikes and roller blades, or limiting ball games to specific areas. Some parks have a ladies' day when entry is restricted to women, girls and young boys.

What *Not* To Wear

Compared to the rest of the GCC, Abu Dhabi is a fairly liberal city that adopts a much more relaxed attitude to what visitors can wear in public. However, there are some rules that apply to dress and beachwear that visitors must follow. Bikinis are fine in private hotel resorts, although string bottoms and going topless is a big no-no – wherever you are in Abu Dhabi. While plenty of beachgoers wear bikinis on public beaches, it can occasionally attract unwanted attention, so best to wear a one piece or sarong while sunbathing or head for a beach park or resort beach. For men, it is worth remembering that some nationalities (and the fashion police) might find Speedos offensive, and avoid going to a nearby cafe or shop without putting a t-shirt on first or you'll be considered rude.

01
On The
Water

With a stunning coastline, calm seas and year-round warm waters, a day out on a boat should appear on any explorer's itinerary. There are several options; from a day of sailing around the islands, to an evening cruise along the Abu Dhabi Corniche – and all of them are wonderfully atmospheric experiences.

Some companies run regular, scheduled trips onboard boats that range from high-speed RIBs to luxurious catamarans serving BBQs and playing music on board. Others charter out boats to private parties for sailing, sightseeing or even fishing trips.

For something a bit different, head to the port area where you can find numerous traditional dhows lined up. Some of these no longer transport goods across the Arabian Gulf but instead combine evening sightseeing tours with Arabian cuisine and onboard entertainment, making for a unique evening out. Companies operating out of Abu Dhabi include Belevari Marine (belevari.com), ART Marine (artmarine.net) and Ocean Active (oceanactive.com).

02

BAKE On Saadiyat Beach

Location Saadiyat Public Beach, Saadiyat Island
Web BAKEuae.com **Times** 8am-8pm
Price Guide Admission Dhs.25,sun lounger Dhs.50 (weekdays),
Dhs.75 (weekends) **Map** 2 p.225

As you walk along the jetty to Saadiyat Public Beach, put your toes into the pristine white sand and gaze across the turquoise waters of the Arabian Sea. And then relax.

This heavenly stretch of beach is all yours to enjoy in luxury beach club style – but without the price tag. Managed by BAKE, you can rent sunloungers with umbrellas for the day, as well as lockers (Dhs.15) and towels (Dhs.10). There are showers, changing rooms and a small shop selling beach essentials, with plans for a beach cafe and non-motorised watersports. Lounge in the sun, splash through the waves of the warm, shallow sea, walk along the beach or work out at the weekly beach yoga classes. From May to October, you can even try to spot turtle nests. For the ultimate indulgence, pop into the neighbouring Park Hyatt for lunch.

For stylish sun-worshippers visit BAKE's Corniche hangouts – at Al Sahil Beach, Family Beach and at Al Bateen Beach. Facilities include sunloungers, cabanas and showers. Perfect for sunsets.

03

Al Nahyan Park

Location Corniche Road
Price Guide Free
Map 3 p.213

Pedal along tree-lined walkways, picnic in the sun, or explore the themed play areas. Skyscrapers are visible in the distance, but there's only verdant nature. There are many reasons why Al Nahyan Park, located along Corniche Road, has become a firm favourite with parents and children alike.

Green areas are set in a landscape of wide walkways, tunnels, water features and landscaping, just minutes from the beach and Corniche. There are age-specific play zones scattered across the park, including a pirate ship, toddler village with toy train and fire engine, and swings, slides and tunnels of all shapes and sizes. The Misty Valley Walk is great fun! Light refreshments are served at a central cafe, and there are plenty of shaded grassy areas and benches to enjoy an ice cream or a BBQ.

Winter weekends find local and expat families spread all over the park, enjoying homemade picnics and beautiful weather. If you want a good spot, make sure you arrive early.

04

Coast Roads

Location Eastern Ringroad to Coast Road
Map 4 p.215

Abu Dhabi island is flanked by the Eastern Ringroad on the north east side and the Coast Road on the south west. You may not expect two of the main arteries connecting the foot of the island with the Corniche and central business district to provide nice outdoor areas. However, just off the sides of these roads – both of which enjoy delightful coastal views – the land has been developed to provide long green strips with barbecue areas, play areas and walking paths.

The coastal flank of the Eastern Ringroad, which looks out over the mangroves, eventually meets the Eastern Mangroves Hotel and Spa by Anantara, where a public path follows the water all the way into town – a great place for a long walk. On the other side of the island, the road leads past the Al Gurm Resort before arriving at Al Bateen Marina.

Al Maya Island Resort

Location Halat Al Bahraini (Al Maya Island)
Web almayaislandresort.ae **Tel** 02 667 7777 **Map** 5 p.210

Al Maya Island Resort is a real undiscovered gem of Abu Dhabi. Located just nine kilometres from the Corniche, you can jump on board a boat at one of the main marinas and be on Al Maya Island in less than 15 minutes. If you do just that, you'll find a beautiful boutique resort at the other end. Operated by Abu Dhabi Country Club, there are six villas and five chalets at the resort, as well as a lagoon-like swimming pool, a restaurant, a huge spa and a watersports centre which offers banana boating, kayaking, wakeboarding, paddle boarding and scuba diving.

Families and couples will both enjoy a visit to Al Maya, but the island's main appeal is for younger holidaymakers – or at least the young at heart. On select Fridays throughout the year, boats leave the Al Maya jetty behind Rotana Khalidiyah Palace and take partygoers out to the island for afternoon beach and pool parties.

06

Fairmont Bab Al Bahr Beach Club

Location Al Maqta **Web** fairmont.com/BabAlBahr
Tel 02 654 3333 **Times** 6am-10pm (daily) **Map** 6 p.217

The Fairmont Bab Al Bahr Beach Club is without doubt one of the best in the capital. The single day rate entitles guests to more than the stretch of immaculate beach, which overlooks the main island and Sheikh Zayed Grand Mosque, with its comfortable range of loungers and recliners; you can also take a dip in the two temperature-controlled pools, lap pool or laze in the poolside Jacuzzi.

You can try your hand at beach football, badminton, Frisbee, softball, volleyball, rugby and even beach bocce. There are also kids' pools and play areas, trampolines, and organised sandcastle building. Throw in the

poolside bar and restaurant, and it's easy to while an entire day away here, soaking up the sun.

07

The Desert

With vast areas of virtually untouched wilderness right the way across the UAE, taking to the desert is a very popular pastime. Every other vehicle on Abu Dhabi's roads seems to be a 4WD but, unlike in many countries where they're reserved for running the kids to school, there is ample opportunity to truly put them to the off-road test in Abu Dhabi.

Dune bashing, or desert driving, is one of the toughest challenges for both car and driver, but, once you have mastered it, it's also the most fun. Those who want to drive themselves should do so in a controlled environment or practise first at OffRoad Zone (offroad-zone.com) in Jebel Ali, on the way to Dubai. If you don't know where to start, or don't want to risk driving yourself, then you should contact one of Abu Dhabi's many tour companies that offer desert and mountain safaris. During the day, combine dune bashing with quad biking, camel riding and lunch, while evening safaris add huge buffets and traditional entertainment to the mix. Some even allow you to camp out beneath the stars.

For a breathtaking aerial tour of the desert, you can also book a Seawings flight. Soar high above the dunes for a truly memorable view.

Breakwater

Location Corniche **Map** 8 p.212

Jutting out from the south west end of the Corniche is the Breakwater where you'll find Marina Mall, but it also provides numerous opportunities for enjoying the fresh air and bright sunlight. For starters, the Breakwater is a great place to go for a stroll, with wide pavements and plenty of places to stop and watch the fishermen who are casting into the Gulf.

Both Abu Dhabi International Marine Sports Club (adimsc.ae) and the Heritage Village make for interesting stops as you walk out to the end of the Breakwater where the giant flagpole stands tall. Marina Cafe and Havana Cafe are located en route, giving you the opportunity to grab a drink and take some great snaps of the view back to the Corniche and the towers that line it.

Finally, if you head up to the west side of Marina Mall, you'll come to Mirage Marine – a Lebanese cafe with a delightful outdoor area where you can eat mezze, smoke shisha and spot dolphins in the lagoon between the Breakwater and Emirates Palace. Above Mirage Marine is Il Porto – an Italian restaurant with a cracking terrace that is also a top alfresco offering.

The Abu Dhabi Theatre building is also worth a look. Next to a towering 123m flagpole, the unmissable building has hosted a number of popular concerts for the Abu Dhabi Classics series.

09

Khalifa Park

Location Shk Zayed Bin Sultan St
Web adm.gov.ae **Times** 8am-10pm
Price Guide Free, Murjan Splash Park Dhs.40 **Map** 9 p.217

It's a good thing that Khalifa Park is the capital's biggest, because it has a lot crammed inside. A library, maritime museum, desert garden centre, miniature railway, and water park are some of the park's permanent attractions, while it has begun to host seasonal events such as a farmers' market, a global shopping festival and a circus inside an amphitheatre.

Despite all of the activities on offer, Khalifa Park doesn't feel crowded or claustrophobic. In fact, it's easy to find some space to call your own alongside the paths, sculptures, and waterfalls. Several park entrances help the crowds thin out even further.

A definite highlight for the under-13 crew is the Murjan Splash Park. With a lazy river, water trampolines, and a mechanical surfboard, this is an aquatic paradise that will make you wish you were a kid all over again.

Saadiyat Beach Club

Location Saadiyat Island **Web** saadiyatbeachclub.ae
Tel 02 656 3500 **Price Guide** Day pass from Dhs.220
Map 10 p.225

The best way to think of Saadiyat Beach Club is as a five-star hotel without the bedrooms; walking into the magnificent lobby, guests are greeted as though they're checking into a luxury beach resort. Also inside, you'll find a fully equipped gym, a coffee lounge, a restaurant and a couple of bars. The lovely amenities include a palatial Jacuzzi, sauna, steam room and day beds for a spot of reading. But the real action is outside the giant lobby windows. Firstly, there's an amazing stretch of attractive beach, with the warm waters of the Gulf lapping up on to the sands. Their inviting pool is huge and surrounded by sumptuous, cabana-style beds and sun loungers. If all those outdoor hours wear you down, head to De La Costa for sustenance, or snacks and drinks can be delivered to wherever you're relaxing. Kids should love it here too; there's a children's pool, as well as an entertaining kids' club for those aged between three and 12. For some downtime, enjoy a sundowner at Cabana9 before dining at the delightful Safina.

YAS ISLAND YOUR TICKET TO A WORLD OF MAGIC

Abu Dhabi Experiences

Abu Dhabi Experiences
Introduction

Over the last few decades, Abu Dhabi has been transformed into a modern metropolis. This global icon is an intoxicating place filled with experiences to match.

Many of Abu Dhabi's most ambitious projects are now recognised all over the world, from the majestic Emirates Palace and the spectacular Aldar HQ 'Pill' building to the awesome Yas Island. Abu Dhabi is a byword for luxurious indulgence, multicultural lifestyles, architectural excess, lavish beach holidays and general fun in the sun, but it is also gaining a reputation for being one of the most diverse tourist destinations on the planet; a place where your appetite can be sated, whether you're into relaxed beach holidays, cultural breaks, activity trips or sporting tours.

And while Abu Dhabi may be many things to many people, there are a few specific activities and experiences that are either unique to the UAE capital, or perfectly sum up a side of the city. The juxtaposition of old and new, the mix of traditional Arabia with the West, is one characteristic that baffles, intrigues and delights visitors and, with that in mind, the various bus and boat tours provide the perfect perspective to take in this contrast. Being in a traditional souk one moment and at the giant Yas Mall the next, is pure Abu Dhabi.

While you're in the mood for touring, a desert safari – which usually comes complete with an Arabian buffet, entertainment and dune bashing – is the kind of experience you'll struggle to find elsewhere; hot air ballooning may

be available in other locations, but doing it as the sun rises over the desert is pretty special.

In terms of modern Abu Dhabi, you'll want to spend some time in the Corniche area, which is home to the beach parks, Etihad Towers (etihadtowers.com) and the Breakwater. But dominating the Corniche is, of course, Emirates Palace and looking out from the terrace of the world's most expensive hotel while sipping on gold-trimmed coffee is an experience that is only available in Abu Dhabi – until someone builds a more expensive and opulent hotel, of course!

Overindulgence is undeniably an Abu Dhabi trait too and there's no doubt that residents and visitors in the city enjoy the finer things in life. Brunch may be available around the world, but the Abu Dhabi brunch is something else entirely. Meanwhile afternoon tea in the city has all the old world charm you'd expect to find in London or Paris, rather than a city in the Middle East.

Taste of Arabia
Tucking into traditional mezze and grilled meats, washing it all down with a fresh fruit juice and finishing your meal with a shisha pipe may not be unique to Abu Dhabi, but it is pure Arabia and the UAE capital has some of the best places to enjoy that traditional experience.

The Corniche

Location Al Khubeirah
Map 1 p.213

The Corniche is the beating heart of the capital, connecting the west of the island to the east of the island but also demarking its main business and tourism areas – it's an area to soak up the charm and atmosphere of modern Abu Dhabi. It's a lovely place for a stroll but the whole Corniche runs some eight kilometres in total; if you want to enjoy the entire length of it, take advantage of the waterfront section which is fully paved, making it ideal for roller blading, jogging or cycling; bikes are available to hire near the Hiltonia Beach Club.

The Corniche Road is lined with the high-rise towers that make up Abu Dhabi's spectacular skyline. The inland side has been beautifully landscaped with parks, small gardens, fountains and covered seating areas that are perfect for a picnic. All areas are easily accessible, with parking and safe pedestrian underpasses.

To see the Corniche from a different perspective, head to the Observation Deck at 300, located in Jumeirah At Etihad Towers. The panoramic vista from 300m up is truly breathtaking, and you'll be able to see most of the city.

O2
Desert Safari

Location Various
Times 3pm-9pm (daily)
Price Guide Around Dhs.200 (adult)

You can go almost anywhere and lie on a beach, laze by the pool, take to the shops and dine at high-end restaurants – what makes a trip to Abu Dhabi truly special are the kinds of experiences that are totally unique to this region. Desert safaris certainly fit that bill.

All of the main tour operators offer very similar packages and you should be able to book directly with your hotel. For the full Arabian experience, book an evening safari – you'll be picked up in a 4WD from your hotel before being whisked away into the desert, where your experienced driver will show you exactly what off-road vehicles were made for.

After the rollercoaster 4WD ride, you'll stop on one of the tallest dunes to watch the sun go down over the vast desertscape. There's time to take your next Facebook profile picture, before you get back into the vehicle to go to a Bedouin-style desert camp. There, you can ride a quad bike, mount a camel, have your hands painted with henna, feast on an Arabian banquet, and enjoy the entertainment – in the form of a traditional belly dancer and a whirling dervish dancer. Finally, pile into the 4WD for the journey back to your hotel.

Friday Brunch

Location Various **Times** 11am–4pm
Price Guide Dhs.95-695

You might think the word 'brunch' is self-explanatory: a portmanteau of 'breakfast' and 'lunch' – a meal you have between the two more accepted dining anchors. If so, you clearly haven't had brunch in Abu Dhabi. Far from the genteel image of croissants, scrambled eggs and coffee over the day's papers, brunch here is synonymous with triumphantly eating your own body weight in food and washing it down with free-flowing champagne. And all for a set price.

The Tavern, Belgian Beer Cafe and Heroes are the spiritual homes of the debauched brunch, while Choices and CuiScene are both child-friendly and a less alcohol-orientated atmosphere. Dusit Thani's Urban Kitchen and Jing Asia offer something a bit different, while Bubbalicious at The Westin and Olea at St Regis epitomise Abu Dhabi's posh and pricey all-inclusive approach; Origins at Yas Viceroy and brunch at P&C by Sergi Arola are high-minded affairs.

Kayaking

Location Eastern Mangroves **Web** noukhada.ae
Tel 02 558 1889 **Times** Various, depending on tour
Price Guide From Dhs.150 **Map** 1 p.215

Escaping to the mangroves that surround Abu Dhabi Island is a tranquil, relaxing way to spend a few hours. Noukhada Adventure Company runs eco-friendly tours with experienced guides who explain the natural fish, birds, mammals and sea creatures that make the mangroves their home. If you are lucky enough to be on tour at high tide, you'll be paddling inside the twisted, tangled channels of the mangrove forest; low-tide tours have to stick to the dredged channels on the outskirts. Single and double kayaks are available, and children as young as three are allowed on board. Paddling your own kayak for the 90 minute tour is a bit of a workout but the utter peace and calm of the mangroves are worth all of the effort you'll expend. Both single and double kayaks are available.

Noukhada also organises BBQ island tours, mystery tours and overnight excursions. A snorkel safari off Ooid Shoals, or a mini mangrove kayak from Yas Beach are other great options for older kids.

05
Boat Racing

It's maybe not the most obvious or globally-popular of spectator sports, but boat racing is an important part of Emirati culture, reflecting the country's close connection with the sea. If you do get the chance to watch, some fantastic racing takes place in Abu Dhabi.

With both the Abu Dhabi Grand Prix in November and then the Dubai Grand Prix in December, the UAE is the only country with two stops in the Class 1 World Power Boating Championship (class-1.com). These boats are something to behold, reaching speeds of 250km/h and sometimes barely even touching the water.

In addition to Class 1 events, there is the F1 Powerboat World Championships, the Wooden Power Boats Championship, the UAE Jet Ski Championships, sailing competitions and dhow races throughout the year at the Abu Dhabi International Marine Sports Club (see adimsc.ae).

For something completely different, however, every year there's the Abu Dubai Dragon Boat Festival in October, (dubaidragonboat.com), with teams from all over the UAE competing in the races.

In January 2012, Abu Dhabi was the first Middle East port ever to host the world's biggest sailing event, the Volvo Ocean Race, which drew huge crowds. The event was hosted again in 2014-2015, and its success just might make it a regular port on the race itinerary.

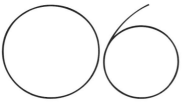

Big Bus Tour

Location Various **Web** bigbustours.com
Tel 02 449 0026 **Times** 9am-5pm (daily)
Price Guide Dhs.220 (adult)

If you only booked a short break in Abu Dhabi, or perhaps are stopping in for a few days en route to another destination, then you'll want to see as much of this incredible city as possible in a short amount of time. The Big Bus Tour is an excellent option for seeing all the highlights in one go. The hop-on hop-off tour knows exactly what tourists want to see. The fleet of air-conditioned double-deckers are fantastic for sightseeing and the rolling multi-lingual commentary is especially useful.

Marina Mall is the main starting point in Abu Dhabi, but riders can get on or off at any of the 21 stops that include Sheikh Zayed Grand Mosque, the Meena souks, the Corniche, Abu Dhabi Mall, the Public Beach and Heritage Village. The stop on Saadiyat Island, is the connection point for a separate Yas shuttle which includes Yas Mall, Ferrari World as well as environmentally friendly Masdar City.

The ticket, which is valid for 24 hours, includes free entry to the Sky Tower viewing platform at Marina Mall, as well as a discount on the Observation Deck at 300 at Jumeirah At Etihad Towers. The Big Bus Company also offers a combined Abu Dhabi/Dubai ticket so that you can explore both cities in two days.

07

Yas Island Weekends

Location Yas Island West
Web yasisland.ae **Map** 7 p.222

The entertainment on Yas Island began with the series of F1 concerts that still accompany the Grand Prix each November and have seen the likes of stars such as Robbie Williams, Coldplay, Eminem, Britney Spears, Paul McCartney, Kylie Minogue, Beyonce, Kanye West, Linkin Park and Prince play over the years.

However, the concerts proved so popular that the organiser, Flash Entertainment, has rolled out other similar events throughout the rest of the year, under the title of Yas Island Show Weekends. Although some parts of the weekend sometimes take place elsewhere, the majority are focused on the du Arena – a state-of-the-art concert pavilion that sits between two of the arms of Ferrari World. The venue even features a cooling system that allows events to be held in the summer months.

Although other events, such as drag racing and basketball, have formed part of the weekends before, they're traditionally music-focused, with Stevie Wonder, Snoop Dogg, Madonna and Shakira all having performed here.

Yas Island hotels offer special discounted rates around concert dates. A visit to Yas should include Ferrari World, Yas Waterworld, Yas Mall and Yas Marina to make it an action-packed weekend.

08

Dhow Dinner Cruise

Location Various
Times 7.30pm-10.30pm (daily)
Price Guide Dhs.120-345

One of the absolute Abu Dhabi must-do experiences for tourists is the dhow dinner cruise, which takes visitors out from the dhow harbour at the eastern end of the Corniche and sails them along the length of the Corniche.

Traditionally trading crafts that ship cargo between the Gulf and Iran, these dhows have been converted to become floating restaurants; the two to three-hour tours typically see diners sit on the top deck, beneath the stars, while an Arabian buffet is served up. Food such as Arabic mezze and mixed grill platters are traditional fare, followed by a dessert of fruit and local sweets.

The cruises take in all the traditional landmarks of the Corniche, giving guests a unique view of the distinctive city skyline. See the domes, towers, and minarets that line the Corniche road, while relaxing at your table or on floor cushions.

Dhow sunset and lunch cruises are also available.

Championship
Golf Courses

Location Various
Times 6am-10pm (daily)
Price Guide Dhs.260-695 (18 holes)

With big names like Gary Player, Peter Harradine and Kyle Phillips all lending their star-power to Abu Dhabi's greens through successful design collaborations, it is little surprise that the popularity of the city as a world-class golf destination has now been cemented. Clubs and societies from all over the world are making the golf tour to Abu Dhabi an integral part of their annual schedules. And the golf is varied; from championship courses to links and beach courses, and even a sand course.

Hotels and tour operators can pre-book your tee times if you're heading over for a golf-heavy few days, or you can contact the courses directly. If you stay at certain hotels, such as the Westin Abu Dhabi Golf Resort & Spa or the hotels on Yas and Saadiyat, you can book packages that include a round or two as well as your room.

Top 10 Golf Courses

Saadiyat Beach Golf Club
Map **11** p.225
sbgolfclub.ae
Yas Links Map **12** p.222
yaslinks.com
Abu Dhabi Golf Club
Map **13** p.218
adgolfclub.com
Abu Dhabi City Golf Club
Map **14** p.214 *adcitygolf.ae*
Emirates Golf Club Map **15** p.211
dubaigolf.com
Dubai Creek Golf & Yacht Club
Map **16** p.211 *dubaigolf.com*
Jumeirah Golf Estates Map **17** p.211
jumeirahgolfestates.com
Montgomerie Golf Club
Map **18** p.211 *themontgomerie.com*
The Els Club Map **19** p.211
elsclubdubai.com
Al Badia Golf Club Map **20** p.211
albadiagolfclub.ae

You may like to time your golf trip to coincide with the Abu Dhabi HSBC Golf Championships (abudhabigolfchampionship.com), a real big hit with fans and merrymakers alike.

10
Architecture

If the name 'United Arab Emirates' has come to stand for any one thing, it is surely architectural excess. While cities across the rest of the world demand practicality of their builders, in Abu Dhabi, architects are encouraged to let their creativity run wild.

In the past, the architectural masterpieces to hit the capital have been bound by a sense of Arabian traditionalism, not that this has prevented either Emirates Palace or Sheikh Zayed Grand Mosque from becoming modern icons of the Middle East. Now, however, Abu Dhabi's most interesting buildings are absolutely modern and bound only by what is and isn't possible.

If you're in the mood for an architectural tour de force, start at the western end of the Corniche with the $5bn Emirates Palace and contrast it with the neighbouring Etihad Towers – the complex of five uber-modern glass skyscrapers that glisten against the blue skies above.

While you're in the mood for stylish skyscrapers, head to the south of the island; there, you'll find a world record breaker high above the vast ADNEC conference centre: Capital Gate is officially the world's most leaning tower, with an 18° slant. Nearby is the recently opened Sheikh Zayed Bridge. This snaking bridge is the third bridge connecting the south of the island with the mainland and was designed by Iraqi-British architect Zaha Hadid.

Off the island, the spherical Aldar HQ (below) – known as 'The Pill' – has to be seen to be believed. And the Guggenheim and Louvre museums on Saadiyat Island are sure to amaze when they open in the near future.

You can see several stunning buildings off the main island too. One such icon is the futuristic Yas Viceroy hotel (*far left*), which glows blue at night and straddles Yas Marina Circuit; it has become one of the most famous structures in sport today.

HUGE FUN
ON YOUR
DOORSTEP

Easy to get to, easy to get around, easy to enjoy. Wild Wadi is all family fun and excitement. Watch the kids shriek and scream their way through the best day of their lives. Book your tickets at **wildwadi.com** or call 04 348 4444

Wild Wadi

WATERPARK

Life. Refreshed.

**15 YEARS
AND STILL
DUBAI'S
FAVORITE**

2014
TRAVELERS'
CHOICE
tripadvisor

Outside Of Abu Dhabi

Beyond

Dubai Skyscrapers

Outside Of Abu Dhabi
Introduction

From the vast Rub Al Khali desert in the south, to the majestic Hajar Mountains in the north, there's an incredible country to visit outside of Abu Dhabi's city limits.

Abu Dhabi may have everything from sports and souks to boutiques and beaches, but there are a number of interesting and varied areas outside of the city borders too; the other emirates in the UAE, as well as the neighbouring country of Oman, all warrant exploration and there's plenty out there to keep you busy.

All six of the other emirates in the UAE – Ajman, Dubai, Fujairah, Ras Al Khaimah, Sharjah and Umm Al Quwain – are within a three-hour drive of central Abu Dhabi. From the sleepy streets of Umm Al Quwain and the rugged mountains of Ras Al Khaimah to the cultural grandiose of Sharjah, each emirate has something different to offer, and each can be explored, at least in part, over a weekend or on a day trip.

Dubai, in particular, should be visited if you have time – ideally for a weekend at least. The drive takes an hour or two, depending on which part of the capital you're leaving from and where in Dubai is your destination. Once there, you're surrounded by essential attractions to explore, from Burj Khalifa (the world's tallest building) and the delightful Dubai Marina (great for an evening stroll), to Mall of the Emirates (with its famous ski slopes), The Dubai Mall and Palm Jumeirah, which is now a must-visit destination in its own right. Plus, you'll find some giant concerts and major international sporting events taking place all throughout the winter months, with the Dubai Rugby Sevens and Dubai World Cup the highlights of the sporting (and social) calendar.

The country's vast deserts and harsh-looking mountains are equally accessible, with a copy of the *UAE Off-Road Explorer*, and can be reached within a couple of hours, if you need to escape civilisation for a while. All of the big tour operators offer one to several day excursions into the mountains or desert, including accommodation that ranges from camping to five-star hotels.

There are also several incredible resort hideaways that combine comfortable lodgings with unique activities; these are well worth a weekend away, if you're planning on spending a week or two in the UAE.

Abu Dhabi's status as an international hub means it's easy to find quick, cheap flights to the neighbouring GCC countries of Oman, Saudi Arabia, Qatar, Bahrain and Kuwait, none of which are more than a 90-minute flight away.

All You Need To Know

In addition to our mini marvel, *Abu Dhabi Visitors' Guide*, Explorer publishes the *UAE Off-Road Explorer*, the *Oman Off-Road Explorer*, the *Ultimate UAE Explorer* and many more amazing titles. If you love the outdoors and exploring, these guides contain everything you need to know. Order your copies online at askexplorer.com/shop or from leading book shops around the UAE.

01

Hatta

Web hattaforthotel.com **Tel** 04 809 9333
Map **1** p.211

Less than an hour from Dubai, Hatta feels a whole world away, making it a great spot for a break from the hustle and bustle. Outside the town, there are plenty of off-roading opportunities, including the Hatta pools where you can take a cooling dip. If you prefer your action on two wheels, then this is also a popular area for cyclists.

Back in town, the Heritage Village is constructed around an old settlement and was restored in the style of a traditional mountain village. Hatta's

history goes back over 3,000 years and the area includes a 200-year-old mosque and a fort, which is now used as a weaponry museum. Hatta Fort Hotel is a secluded retreat featuring 50 chalet-style suites which come with patios overlooking the Hajar Mountains and the tranquil gardens; the hotel also doubles as the area's main activity provider, with swimming pools, floodlit tennis courts, mini-golf and a driving range, as well as an archery range (instruction is available).

Oman

Web oman.com
Map 2 p.211

The most accessible country from the UAE, Oman is a peaceful and breath-taking destination, with history, culture and spectacular scenery to spare. The capital, Muscat, has enough attractions to keep you busy for a long weekend, with beautiful beaches, great restaurants and cafes, the mesmerising old souk at Mutrah, and the Sultan Qaboos Mosque.

Outside the capital are many historic towns and forts. You'll also discover some of the most stunning mountain and wadi scenery in the Middle East, with the region's highest peaks begging to be explored by hikers and mountain bikers. Salalah, in the south of Oman, has the added bonus of being cool and wet even during the summer months, which gives it a very different appearance to the rest of the Arabian Peninsula.

The drive from Abu Dhabi to Muscat takes just five hours, or you can hop on a flight from Abu Dhabi to Muscat which takes just an hour.

O3

Dubai

Web dubai.ae **Map** 3 p.211

Cliches tend to trip off the tongue when describing Abu Dhabi's little brother – the city of gold, sleepy fishing village transformed into modern metropolis, the Vegas of the Middle East, and so on. The truth is that, while the emirate boasts an incredible number of attractions claiming to be the tallest, biggest or longest, it's not all bright lights. The atmospheric old town around the Creek, and the restored Al Fahidi Historic District (formerly Bastakiya) are must-sees for any visitor. The beautiful Jumeirah Mosque is one of the few mosques in the region open to non-Muslims, offering a rare chance to learn about the impact of Islam on the local people.

If it is bright lights you're after, then you'll find plenty of this in Dubai. From skiing on real snow at Ski Dubai and plunging through shark-infested waters at Aquaventure at Atlantis, The Palm, to shopping till you drop at The Dubai Mall and surveying the city from the world's tallest building, Burj Khalifa, a weekend trip to Dubai promises an action-packed, once-in-a-lifetime break.

Beyond the city, the desert opens up further possibilities and many visitors choose to combine a city break with a couple of nights camping with a tour group, or relaxing at a luxury desert resort such as Al Maha Desert Resort & Spa or Bab Al Shams. The endless list of five-star hotels, restaurants, bars and clubs will ensure a well fed and watered stay, and luxury spas and clean beaches provide ample opportunities to relax while in Dubai.

For heritage and a glimpse into Dubai's past, Al Fahidi Historic District's narrow streets and souks are not to be missed. Dubai Museum, housed in a charming fort, charts the city's growth, but don't leave without crossing Dubai Creek on an abra (wooden boat).

Sir Bani Yas is the UAE's biggest natural island, lying just nine kilometres offshore. It is one of the Desert Islands – a collection of eight protected islands that are being developed for eco-tourism.

It was the late Sheikh Zayed who turned Sir Bani Yas Island into Arabia's largest nature reserve as a way of protecting many natural species. The island plays a key role in conservation, with some 10,000 animals a year from Sir Bani Yas being released back into the wild.

04 Al Ain

Location 160km east of the capital, Abu Dhabi
Web abudhabi.ae **Map 4** p.211

The capital of the eastern region and Abu Dhabi emirate's second city, Al Ain's greenery and the fact that it is the birthplace and childhood home of Sheikh Zayed bin Sultan Al Nahyan, the former (and much-loved) ruler of the UAE, gives it special status in the hearts and minds of Emiratis.

It takes an hour and a half by car to get there and most tour companies offer excursions to this fascinating 'Garden City' that straddles the border with Oman; the UAE side is known as Al Ain and the Oman side as Buraimi.

As a destination, Al Ain combines the old with the new. The city's archaeological legacy is of such significance that Al Ain is now a UNESCO World Heritage Site, with the 18 fortresses around the city and the seven natural oases all demanding exploration; the oasis palm plantations provide welcome shade and a haven from the city. On the outskirts of Al Ain, you will also find a Camel & Livestock Souk (adach. ae) which is worth a visit. Just outside the city, you'll find the mountain of Jebel Hafeet and Al Ain Zoo.

> For those who like their thrills and spills, there's Wadi Adventure, karting at Al Ain Raceway (alainraceway.com), and rides for all the family at Hili Fun City.

05

The Pearl Coast

Location West of Abu Dhabi, from Mirfa to Jebel Dhanna
Map 5 p.210

The coastline that stretches west from Abu Dhabi towards the Saudi border is actually some of the least explored terrain by both tourists and residents – a shame as it's where you'll find charming towns and, most significantly, wide golden beaches with turquoise lagoons.

About 140km west of Abu Dhabi is Mirfa – a small, quiet coastal town with a long stretch of beach that is a kitesurfer's paradise. Many choose to pitch tents right on the beach, especially during the popular Al Gharbia Watersports Festival that takes place in March or April each year. The event is a weekend of fireworks, competitive kitesurfing, wakeboarding and kayaking. The

Mirfa Hotel (almarfapearlhotels.com) is a nice beach resort, with a couple of restaurants and bars to choose from, as well as a wide range of watersports on offer.

Located two hours west of Abu Dhabi, Jebel Dhanna is a great coastal getaway. With a sandy beach and clear, shallow sea, it is one of the region's best kept secrets.

There are two hotels here: the plush five-star Danat Jebel Dhanna Resort (danathotels.com) and the Dhafra Beach Hotel (danathotels.com). Jebel Dhanna is also a good base for boat trips out to some of the islands, such as Dalma Island, as well as the departure point for some incredible scuba diving adventures.

06
Liwa Oasis

Location Al Gharbia, Western Region
Map 6 p.210

If you love the great outdoors, you're simply going to love the Liwa Oasis. Jump in a 4WD and prepare yourself for the most adventurous off-road driving the UAE has to offer, and some of its most incredible scenery. Liwa is located on the edge of the Empty Quarter (or Rub Al Khali) and is a must for any off-roader or adventurer during their time in the Middle East.

Stretching into Oman, Yemen and Saudi Arabia, the Empty Quarter is the biggest sand desert on the planet, and the sheer scale of the scenery and the size of the dunes, which rise to heights of over 300 metres, has to be seen to be believed.

The Liwa area is home to one of the largest oases on the Arabian Peninsula which stretches over 150 kilometres and provides a surprising amount of greenery. While the main feature of Liwa is the desert, there are also several other attractions which are worth exploring along the way, including tiny villages, a fish farm and some recently renovated forts. They are all interesting places to poke around in for an idea of what life used to be like in this remote corner of the country.

To access the biggest dunes and witness spectacular sunrises, camping is the most practical accommodation option. However, if home comforts are a necessity, try the family-friendly Tilal Liwa Hotel (tilalliwa.danathotels.com) which sits on the edge of the desert or, alternatively, the stunning five-star Qasr Al Sarab Desert Resort by Anantara on the edge of the unspoilt Liwa crescent.

07

Fujairah

Location Nr The Gulf Of Oman **Web** fujairah.ae
Tel 09 222 2111 **Map** 7 p.211

A trip to the east coast is a must for any west coast tourist wanting a slower, more authentic slice of Emirati life. Made up of the emirate of Fujairah and several enclaves belonging to Sharjah, the villages along the east coast sit between the rugged Hajar Mountains and the gorgeous Gulf of Oman.

The real draw here is the landscape. The surrounding hillsides are dotted with ancient forts and watchtowers, which add an air of charm. Off the coast, the seas and coral reefs make a great spot for fishing, diving and watersports, and the wadis, forts, waterfalls and even natural hot springs are fun to explore.

08

Northern Emirates

Location Ajman, Ras Al Khaimah, Sharjah and Umm Al Quwain
Map 8 p.211

The Northern Emirates is the collective term given for Ajman, Ras Al Khaimah, Sharjah and Umm Al Quwain, which lie to the north of Dubai – and there's plenty to discover.

Sharjah is the UAE's cultural capital, with an eclectic mix of museums, heritage preservation and souks. The surrounding Buheirah Corniche is popular for evening strolls.

Umm Al Quwain is probably best known for Dreamland – the country's

original waterpark with views over a beautiful lagoon and flamingos. For a quirky experience, you can stay in cabins or tents within Dreamland.

With the Hajar Mountains rising just behind the city, the Arabian Gulf and the desert, Ras Al Khaimah has possibly the best scenery of any emirate. The terrain begs to be explored by intrepid sorts, while the forts and museums are also well worth checking out.

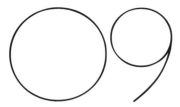

09

Emirates National Auto Museum

Location E65 Rd/Hamim Rd **Web** enam.ae
Tel 050 829 3952 **Times** 9am-1pm, 2pm-6pm (daily)
Price Guide Dhs.10 **Map** 9 p.211

In spite of all the money that has been spent on big, bright attractions, occasionally in the UAE it is still possible to stumble upon something that is totally unexpected – and all the better for it. The Emirates National Auto Museum certainly falls into that category, providing something of a bizarre counterpoint to Yas Island's Ferrari World.

Located 45km south of Abu Dhabi, an impressive pyramid rises from the desert. Inside is an incredible assortment of cars belonging to one collector: Sheikh Hamad bin Hamdan Al Nahyan, aka the 'Rainbow Sheikh'. This includes the Sheikh's rainbow Mercedes collection.

Opened in 2005, the museum is now home to almost 200 cars, including a vast collection of off-road vehicles, classic American cars, and the largest truck in the world. Some exhibits were showcased in the BBC TV programme Top Gear.

Even if you're not particularly interested in cars, this is a fascinating vintage collection and the globe caravan alone is worth the visit. The museum is an ideal detour on the journey to Liwa.

10

Al Maha Desert Resort & Spa

Location Dubailand **Web** al-maha.com
Tel 04 832 9900 **Map** 10 p.211

Calling Al Maha a hotel is a bit like calling the Rub Al Khali a bit of sand – this desert getaway is something else entirely and, if a few days here don't blow your mind, then we're not sure what will. Al Maha has been designed to resemble a typical Bedouin camp, but conditions are anything but basic. Each suite is beautifully crafted and has its own private pool and butler service.

There is a superb Timeless Spa on site, as well as The Terrace Bar and the excellent Al Diwaan restaurant, although most guests opt to have their meals served on their private decking – and why not? Especially when each room looks out on to the Dubai Desert Conservation Reserve with picturesque dunes, antelopes and Arabian red foxes to admire.

there's more to life...

The Region's Best Maps

Maps

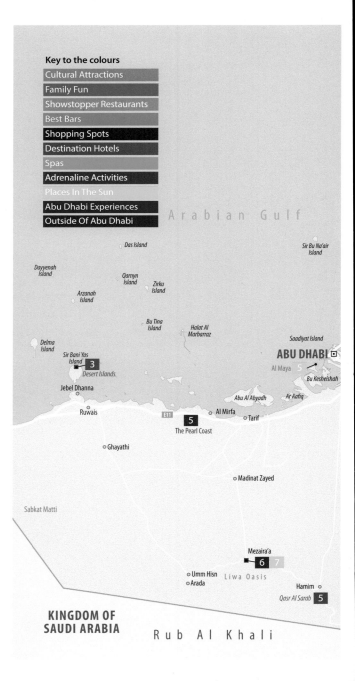

Key to the colours

Cultural Attractions
Family Fun
Showstopper Restaurants
Best Bars
Shopping Spots
Destination Hotels
Spas
Adrenaline Activities
Places In The Sun
Abu Dhabi Experiences
Outside Of Abu Dhabi

Arabian Gulf

Das Island

Sir Bu Na'air Island

Dayyenah Island

Qarnyn Island

Zirku Island

Arzanah Island

Bu Tina Island

Halat Al Marbarraz

Delma Island

Saadiyat Island

Sir Bani Yas Island **3**

ABU DHABI ⊡

Al Maya **5**

Desert Islands

Bu Kesheishah

Jebel Dhanna

Abu Al Abyadh   *Ar Aafiq*

Ruwais

E11   *Al Mirfa*   *Tarif*

5

The Pearl Coast

○ Ghayathi

○ Madinat Zayed

Sabkat Matti

Mezaira'a

6 7

○ Umm Hisn   Liwa Oasis
○ Arada

Hamim ○

Qasr Al Sarab **5**

KINGDOM OF SAUDI ARABIA   Rub Al Khali

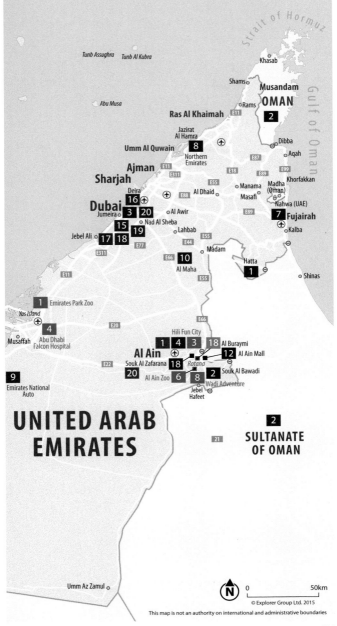

Tunb Assughra   Tunb Al Kubra

Abu Musa

Khasab

Shams

Rams

Musandam
OMAN

2

Dibba

Aqah

Ras Al Khaimah E11

Jazirat
Al Hamra

Umm Al Quwain **8**

Northern
Emirates

Ajman E11

Sharjah E311

Manama

Masafi

Madha
(Oman)

Nahwa (UAE)

Khorfakkan

E18

E89

E99

E55

Deira
16

Al Dhaid

E88

Dubai **3** **20**

7 **Fujairah**

Kalba

Jumeira

Al Awir

15

Nad Al Sheba

Jebel Ali   **17** **18** **19**

Lahbab

E44

E77

Madam

E66 **10**

Al Maha

E55

Hatta

1

Shinas

E311

E11

1 Emirates Park Zoo

Yas Island

4

Musaffah

Abu Dhabi
Falcon Hospital

E20

E66

Hili Fun City

1 **4** **3**   **18** Al Buraymi

12 Al Ain Mall

E22

Al Ain

Souk Al Zafarana

20 **18** *Rotana*

2 Souk Al Bawadi

6 **8** Wadi Adventure

Al Ain Zoo

Jebel
Hafeet

9

Emirates National
Auto

UNITED ARAB
EMIRATES

2

21

SULTANATE
OF OMAN

Umm Az Zamul

N   0   50km

© Explorer Group Ltd. 2015

This map is not an authority on international and administrative boundaries

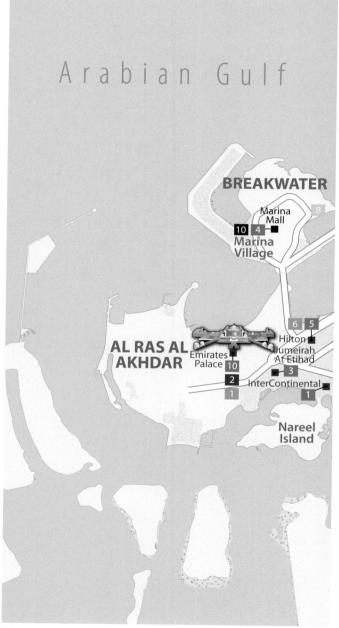

Arabian Gulf

BREAKWATER

Marina
Mall

10 4

**Marina
Village**

6 5

Hilton

**AL RAS AL
AKHDAR**

Jumeirah
At Etihad

Emirates
Palace 10

3

2

InterContinental

1

**Nareel
Island**

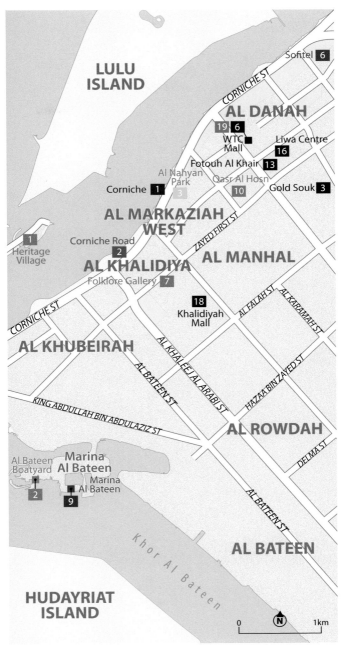

LULU ISLAND

Sofitel 6

CORNICHE ST

AL DANAH

19 6
WTC Mall

Liwa Centre 16

Fotouh Al Khair 13

Al Nahyan Park 3

Qasr Al Hosn 10

Corniche 1

Gold Souk 3

AL MARKAZIAH WEST

ZAYED FIRST ST

1
Heritage Village

Corniche Road 2

AL MANHAL

AL KHALIDIYA

Folklore Gallery 7

18
Khalidiyah Mall

AL FALAH ST

AL KARAMAH ST

CORNICHE ST

AL KHUBEIRAH

AL KHALEEJ AL ARABI ST

AL BATEEN ST

HAZAA BIN ZAYED ST

KING ABDULLAH BIN ABDULAZIZ ST

AL ROWDAH

DELMA ST

Al Bateen Boatyard

Marina Al Bateen

2

Marina Al Bateen

9

AL BATEEN ST

AL BATEEN

Khor Al Bateen

HUDAYRIAT ISLAND

0   1km
N

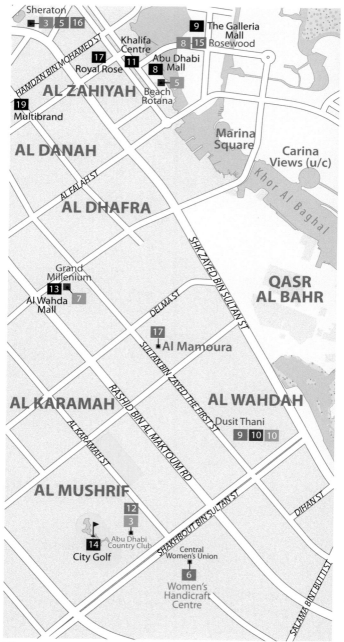

Sheraton
3 5 16

Khalifa
Centre

9 The Galleria
8 15 Mall
Rosewood

17 Abu Dhabi
Royal Rose 11 8 Mall
5

AL ZAHIYAH Beach
Rotana

19
Multibrand

AL DANAH

Marina
Square

Carina
Views (u/c)

AL FALAH ST

Khor Al Baghal

AL DHAFRA

SHK ZAYED BIN SULTAN ST

QASR
AL BAHR

Grand
Millenium
13
7
Al Wahda
Mall

DELMA ST

17
Al Mamoura

SULTAN BIN ZAYED THE FIRST ST

AL KARAMAH

RASHID BIN AL MAKTOUM RD

AL WAHDAH

Dusit Thani
9 10 10

AL KARAMAH ST

AL MUSHRIF

SHAKHBOUT BIN SULTAN ST

DIHAN ST

12
3

14
City Golf

Abu Dhabi
Country Club

Central
Women's Union

6
Women's
Handicraft
Centre

SALAMA BINT BUTTI ST

HAMDAN BIN MOHAMED ST

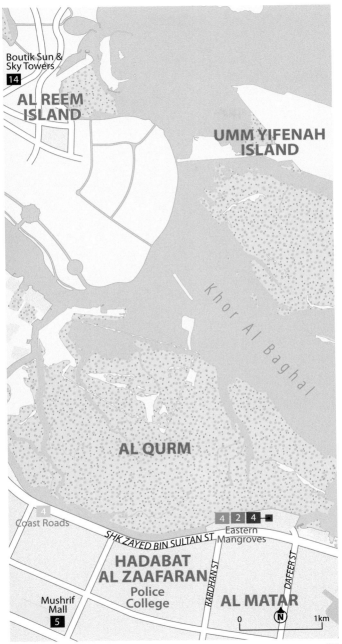

Boutik Sun &
Sky Towers
14

**AL REEM
ISLAND**

**UMM YIFENAH
ISLAND**

Khor Al Baghal

AL QURM

4 **2** **4** ◼

4
Coast Roads

SHK ZAYED BIN SULTAN ST

Eastern
Mangroves

RABDHAN ST

DAFEER ST

**HADABAT
AL ZAAFARAN**
Police
College

Mushrif
Mall
5

AL MATAR

0   1km
Ⓝ

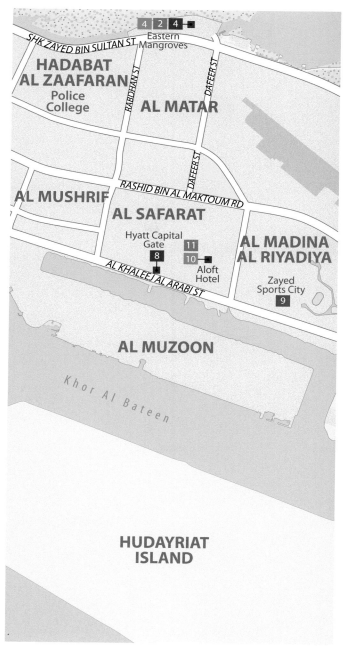

SHK ZAYED BIN SULTAN ST

4 2 4

Eastern
Mangroves

**HADABAT
AL ZAAFARAN**

Police
College

RABDHAN ST

DAFEER ST

AL MATAR

AL MUSHRIF

RASHID BIN AL MAKTOUM RD

DAFEER ST

AL SAFARAT

Hyatt Capital
Gate

11

8

10

Aloft
Hotel

**AL MADINA
AL RIYADIYA**

Zayed
Sports City

9

AL KHALEEJ AL ARABI ST

AL MUZOON

Khor Al Bateen

**HUDAYRIAT
ISLAND**

216

Abu Dhabi Top 10

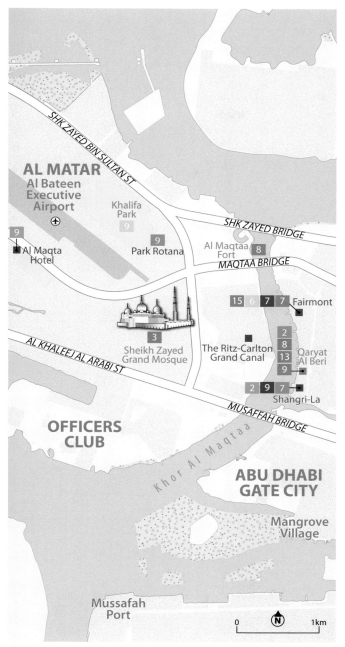

AL MATAR

SHK ZAYED BIN SULTAN ST

Al Bateen
Executive
Airport

Khalifa
Park
9

9
Al Maqta
Hotel

9
Park Rotana

SHK ZAYED BRIDGE

Al Maqtaa
Fort   8

MAQTAA BRIDGE

15 6 7 7 Fairmont

AL KHALEEJ AL ARABI ST

3

Sheikh Zayed
Grand Mosque

The Ritz-Carlton
Grand Canal

2
8
13 Qaryat
9   Al Beri

2 9 7
Shangri-La

MUSAFFAH BRIDGE

OFFICERS
CLUB

Khor Al Maqtaa

ABU DHABI
GATE CITY

Mangrove
Village

Mussafah
Port

0   N   1km

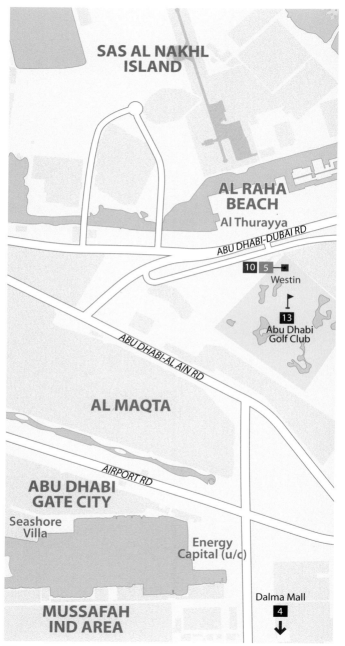

SAS AL NAKHL
ISLAND

AL RAHA
BEACH

Al Thurayya

ABU DHABI-DUBAI RD

`10` `5`

Westin

`13`
Abu Dhabi
Golf Club

ABU DHABI-AL AIN RD

AL MAQTA

AIRPORT RD

ABU DHABI
GATE CITY

Seashore
Villa

Energy
Capital (u/c)

MUSSAFAH
IND AREA

Dalma Mall

`4`
↓

AL RAHA BEACH

Al Rumaila

Al Rumaila

Al Raha
Beach

Al Zahiya

Al Raha
Beach Village

Al Lissaily

Al Shaleela

ABU DHABI-DUBAI RD

Ripe Market
17

Al Raha
Gardens

KHALIFA
CITY

Al Forsan
10

AIRPORT RD

ABU DHABI-AL AIN RD

ZAYED CITY

0   N   1km

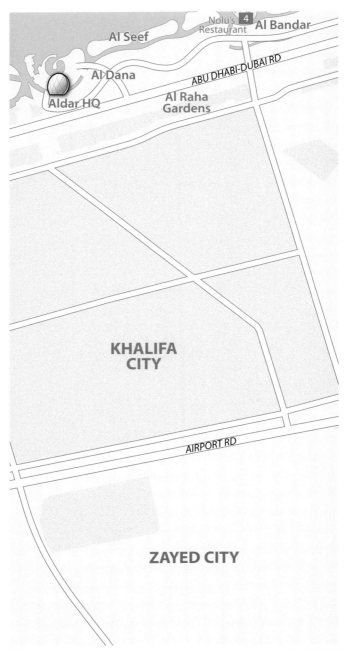

Al Seef

Nolu's
Restaurant **4** Al Bandar

Al Dana

ABU DHABI-DUBAI RD

Aldar HQ

Al Raha
Gardens

**KHALIFA
CITY**

AIRPORT RD

ZAYED CITY

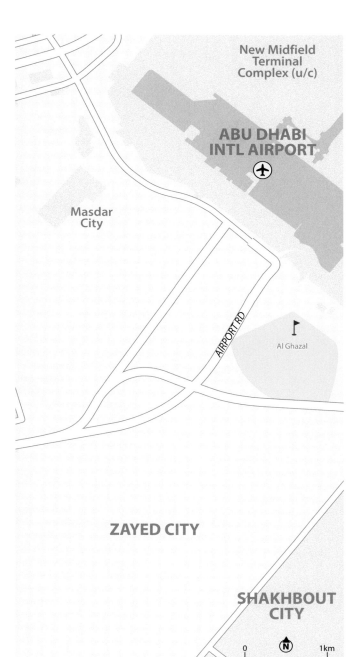

New Midfield
Terminal
Complex (u/c)

**ABU DHABI
INTL AIRPORT**

Masdar
City

AIRPORT RD

Al Ghazal

ZAYED CITY

**SHAKHBOUT
CITY**

0   N   1km

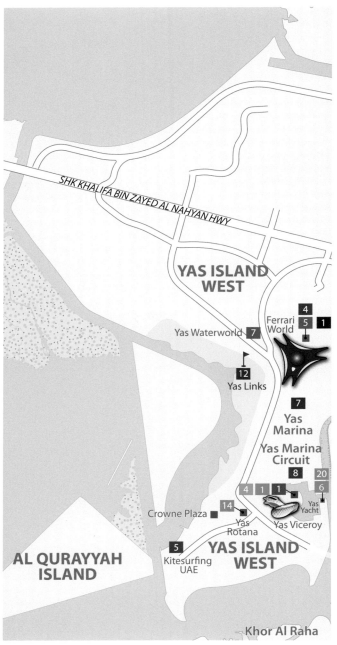

SHK KHALIFA BIN ZAYED AL NAHYAN HWY

YAS ISLAND WEST

Ferrari World **4**
5 **1**

Yas Waterworld **7**

12
Yas Links

7
Yas Marina

Yas Marina Circuit

8
20

4 **1** **1** **6**
Yas Yacht

Crowne Plaza **14**
Yas Rotana

Yas Viceroy

5
Kitesurfing UAE

YAS ISLAND WEST

AL QURAYYAH ISLAND

Khor Al Raha

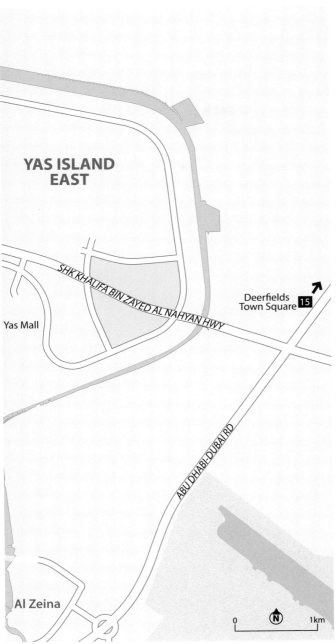

YAS ISLAND
EAST

SHK KHALIFA BIN ZAYED AL NAHYAN HWY

Yas Mall

Deerfields
Town Square 15

ABU DHABI-DUBAI RD

Al Zeina

0   N   1km

Arabian Gulf

SAADIYAT
CULTURAL
DISTRICT

AL MEENA

Fish, Fruit &
Vegetable Market
7

SHEIKH KHALIFA BRIDGE

Al Meena
Port
4

E12

Iranian
Souk
8

Central Business
District

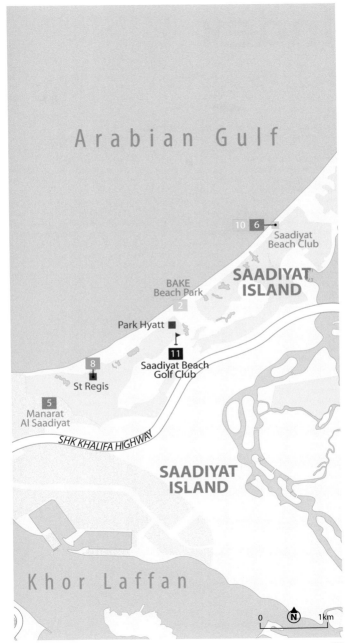

Arabian Gulf

10 6 Saadiyat
Beach Club

SAADIYAT
ISLAND

BAKE
Beach Park
2

Park Hyatt

11

8 Saadiyat Beach
Golf Club

St Regis

5
Manarat
Al Saadiyat

SHK KHALIFA HIGHWAY

SAADIYAT
ISLAND

Khor Laffan

0   N   1km

Index

USEFUL NUMBERS

Embassies & Consulates

Australia	02 401 7500
Bahrain	02 665 7500
Canada	02 694 0300
Czech Republic (Embassy)	02 678 2800
China	02 443 4276
Egypt	02 813 7000
Finland	02 632 8927
France	02 813 1000
Germany	02 644 6693
India	02 449 2700
Iran	02 444 7618
Ireland	02 495 8200
Italy	02 443 5622
Japan	02 443 5696
Jordan	02 444 7100
Kuwait	02 447 7146
Lebanon	02 449 2100
Malaysia	02 448 2775
New Zealand	02 441 1222
The Netherlands	02 695 8000
Oman	02 446 3333
Pakistan	02 444 7800
Philippines	02 639 0006
Poland	02 446 5200
Qatar	02 449 3300
Russia	02 672 1797
Saudi Arabia	02 444 5700
South Africa	02 447 3446
Spain	02 626 9544
Sri Lanka	02 631 6444
Sweden	02 417 8800
Switzerland	02 627 4636
Syria	02 444 8768
Thailand	02 557 6551
UK	02 610 1100
USA	02 414 2200
Yemen	02 444 8457

Emergency Services

Abu Dhabi Police	999
Ambulance	999
Fire Department	997
AAA (Roadside Assistance)	800 8181

24-Hour Pharmacies

Sheikh Khalifa Medical City ER Pharmacy	02 819 2188
Lifeline Hospital Pharmacy	02 633 3340
Al Noor Hospital Pharmacy	02 613 9100
Al Ain Hospital Pharmacy	03 763 5888
Liwa Hospital Pharmacy	02 882 2204

A&E Departments

Al Ain Hospital	03 763 5888
Al Noor Hospital	02 626 5265
Al Rahba Hospital	02 506 4444
Al Salama Hospital	02 696 6777
Corniche Hospital	02 672 4900
Emirates International Hospital	03 763 7777
Hospital Franco-Emirien	02 626 5722
Madinat Zayed Hospital	02 884 4444
Mafraq Hospital	02 501 1111
National Hospital	02 671 1000
NMC Specialty Hospital	02 633 2255
Oasis Hospital	03 722 1251
Sheikh Khalifa Medical City	02 610 2000
Tawam Hospital	03 767 7444

Taxi Services

Al Ghazal Transport	02 444 7787
Al Ghazal Transport	03 751 6565
Arabia Taxi	800 272 242
CARS Taxi	800 227 789
National Taxi	600 543 322
Tawasul Transport	02 673 4444
Tawasul Transport	03 782 5553
TransAD	600 535 353

Airport Info

Etihad Airways	02 511 0000
Emirates Airline	600 55 55 55
Abu Dhabi International Airport Help Desk	02 505 5555
Flight Information	02 575 7500
Baggage Services	02 505 2771

Directory

Abu Dhabi Municipality	800 555
Abu Dhabi Police	02 699 9999
Al Ain Police	03 715 1100
UAE Country Code	+971
Abu Dhabi Area Code	02
Weather	02 666 7776
du Contact Centre (mobile enquiries)	
From mobile	155
From any UAE phone	800 155
du Contact Centre (home enquiries)	04 390 5555
Directory Enquiries (du)	199
Directory Enquiries (Etisalat)	181
Etisalat Customer Care	101
Mobile Phone Code (du)	052/055
Mobile Phone Code (Etisalat)	050/056
Speaking Clock	141
Traffic Police Dept	02 895 5111

BASIC ARABIC

General

Yes	*na'am*
No	*la*
Please	*min fadlak (m)*
	min fadliki (f)
Thank you	*shukran*
Please (in offering)	*tafaddal (m)*
	tafaddali (f)
Praise be to God	*al-hamdu l-illah*
God willing	*in shaa'a l-laah*

Greetings

Greeting (peace be upon you)	*as-salaamu alaykom*
Greeting (in reply)	*wa alaykom is salaam*
Good morning	*sabah il-khayr*
Good morning (in reply)	*sabah in-nuwr*
Good evening	*masa il-khayr*
Good evening (in reply)	*masa in-nuwr*
Hello	*marhaba*
Hello (in reply)	*marhabtayn*
How are you?	*kayf haalak (m)/*
	kayf haalik (f)
Fine, thank you	*zayn, shukran (m)/*
	zayna, shukran (f)
Welcome	*ahlan wa sahlan*
Welcome (in reply)	
	ahlan fiyk (m) / ahlan fiyki (f)
Goodbye	*ma is-salaama*

Introductions

My name is...	*ismiy…*
What is your name?	*shuw ismak (m)/*
	shuw ismik (f)
Where are you from?	
	min wayn inta (m) / min wayn inti (f)
I am from…	*anaa min…*
America	*ameriki*
Britain	*braitani*
Europe	*oropi*
India	*al hindi*

Questions

How many / much?	*kam?*
Where?	*wayn?*
When?	*mataa?*
Which?	*ayy?*
How?	*kayf?*
What?	*shuw?*
Why?	*laysh?*
Who?	*miyn?*
To/for	*ila*

In/at	*fee*
From	*min*
And	*wa*
Also	*kamaan*
There isn't	*maa fee*

Taxi Or Car Related

Is this the road to...	*hadaa al tariyq ila...*
Stop	*kuf*
Right	*yamiyn*
Left	*yassar*
Straight ahead	*siydaa*
North	*shamaal*
South	*januwb*
East	*sharq*
West	*garb*
Turning	*mafraq*
First	*awwal*
Second	*thaaniy*
Road	*tariyq*
Street	*shaaria*
Roundabout	*duwwaar*
Signals	*ishaara*
Close to	*qarib min*
Petrol station	*mahattat betrol*
Sea/beach	*il bahar*
Mountain/s	*jabal/jibaal*
Desert	*al sahraa*
Airport	*mataar*
Hotel	*funduq*
Restaurant	*mata'am*
Slow down	*schway schway*

Accidents & Emergencies

Police	*al shurtaa*
Permit/licence	*rukhsaa*
Accident	*haadith*
Papers	*waraq*
Insurance	*ta'miyn*
Sorry	*aasif (m) / aasifa (f)*

Numbers

Zero	*sifr*
One	*waahad*
Two	*ithnayn*
Three	*thalatha*
Four	*arba'a*
Five	*khamsa*
Six	*sitta*
Seven	*saba'a*
Eight	*thamaanya*
Nine	*tiss'a*
Ten	*ashara*
Hundred	*miya*
Thousand	*alf*

Explorer Products

Residents' Guides

Mini Visitors' Guides

Photography Books & Calendars

Check out ask**explorer**.com/shop

Maps

Adventure & Lifestyle Guides

Apps & eBooks
+ Also available as applications.
* Now available in eBook format.
Visit askexplorer.com/shop

Abu Dhabi Top 10 – 2nd Edition

Lead Editor Lisa Crowther
Editorial Team Lisa Crowther, Julie Hayes
Research Manager Mimi Stankova
Sales Bryan Anes, Sabrina Ahmed
Design Ieyad Charaf, Jayde Fernandes
Maps Zain Madathil, Hidayath Rasi
Photography Henry Hilos, Ieyad Charaf, Pamela Grist,
Pete Maloney, Victor Romero, Hardy Mendrofa

Publishing
Chief Content Officer & Founder Alistair MacKenzie

Editorial & Research
Sr. Corporate Editor Julie Hayes
Consumer Editor Lisa Crowther
Research Manager Mimi Stankova
Researchers Maria Luisa Reyes, Lara Santizo,
Jacqueline Reyes
Production Controller Jaja Lasagas

Design & Photography
Art Director Ieyad Charaf
Layout Manager Jayde Fernandes
Designer M. Shakkeer, Mohamed Abdo
Junior Designer Niyasuthin Batcha
Cartography Manager Zain Madathil
Cartographers Noushad Madathil, Hidayath Rasi
Photography & Gallery Manager Pamela Grist
Photographer & Image Editor Hardy Mendrofa

Media Sales
Director of Sales Peter Saxby
Media Sales Area Managers Laura Zuffa,
Sabrina Ahmed, Bryan Anes
Business Development Managers Pouneh Hafizi,
Sally Koornneef

Retails Sales
Director of Retail Ivan Rodrigues
Retail Sales Specialist Michelle Mascarenhas
Retail Sales Area Supervisors Ahmed Mainodin,
Firos Khan
Retail Sales Merchandisers Johny Mathew,
Shan Kumar, Mehmood Ullah
Retail Sales Drivers Shabsir Madathil,
Nimicias Arachchige
Warehouse Assistant Mohamed Haji, Jithinraj M

Marketing
Marketing Manager Alba Oliveras

Finance, HR & Administration
Accountant Cherry Enriquez
Accounts Assistants Sunil Suvarna,
Jayleen Aguinaldo
Administration Joy H. San Buenaventura
Reception Jayfee Manseguiao
Delivery Driver & PRO Imran Mhalunkar
Office Assistant Shafeer Ahamed

IT & Digital Solutions
Web Developer Waqas Razzaq
IT Manager R. Ajay
Database Programmer Pradeep T.P.

How can we help you?

Ask Explorer
ask**explorer**.com
Log onto our website for great competitions
and essential information about your city and
other places across the Middle East.

Media sales
sales@ask**explorer**.com
Contact us for details of our advertising
rates, corporate bulk sales, online marketing
packages, content licensing and customised
wall maps.

Corporate sales
corporate@ask**explorer**.com
For all your corporate needs, Explorer offers
contract publishing, mapping solutions,
corporate gifts, bespoke content solutions,
customised dust jackets and a wide range of
digital options.

Retail sales
retail@ask**explorer**.com
Talk to us about Explorer's retail sales options,
distribution services and E-shop orders.

General enquiries
info@ask**explorer**.com
Call us on +971 (0)4 340 8805 as we'd love to
hear your thoughts and answer any questions
you might have about this book or any
Explorer products.

Careers
jobs@ask**explorer**.com
Send us your CV if you are talented,
adventurous, knowledgeable, curious,
passionate, creative and above all fun.

Explorer Publishing & Distribution
PO Box 34275, Dubai, United Arab Emirates
Phone: +971 (0)4 340 8805
Fax: +971 (0)4 340 8806

explorerpublishing.com

 /ask**explorer**